Guiding Light

Focusing on the Word
CYCLE B

D0830582

Homilies by Fr. Joe Robinson

Shepherds of Christ Publications
P.O. Box 627
China, Indiana 47250 USA

Toll free USA: (888) 211-3041
Tel: (812) 273-8405
Fax: (812) 273-3182
Email: info@sofc.org
http://www.sofc.org

First Printing: 2008

In honor
of our
Beloved Priests

Table of Contents
Cycle B

Foreward

1st Sunday of Advent
November 27, 2005 1

2nd Sunday of Advent
December 4, 2005 4

Feast of the Immaculate Conception
December 8, 2005 6

3rd Sunday of Advent
December 11, 2005 8

4th Sunday of Advent
December 18, 2005 10

Christmas
December 25, 2005 13

Mary, Mother of God
January 1, 2006 16

Feast of the Epiphany
January 8, 2006 19

2nd Sunday in Ordinary Time
January 15, 2006 22

3rd Sunday in Ordinary Time
January 22, 2006 24

4th Sunday in Ordinary Time
January 29, 2006 27

5th Sunday in Ordinary Time
February 5, 2006 31

6th Sunday in Ordinary Time
February 12, 2006 34

7th Sunday in Ordinary Time
   February 19, 2006 37
8th Sunday in Ordinary Time
   February 26, 2006 40
1st Sunday of Lent
   March 5, 2006 43
2nd Sunday of Lent
   March 12, 2006 45
3rd Sunday of Lent
   March 19, 2006 48
4th Sunday of Lent
   March 26, 2006 51
5th Sunday of Lent
   April 2, 2006 55
Passion Sunday
   April 9, 2006 57
Holy Thursday
   April 13, 2006 60
Easter
   April 16, 2006 63
Second Sunday of Easter
   April 23, 2006 66
Third Sunday of Easter
   April 30, 2006 69
Fourth Sunday of Easter
   May 7, 2006 72
Fifth Sunday of Easter
   May 14, 2006 74
Sixth Sunday of Easter
   May 21, 2006 77
Feast of the Ascension
   May 28, 2006 80

Pentecost
    June 4, 2006 84
Trinity Sunday
    June 11, 2006 86
The Body and Blood of Christ
    June 18, 2006 90
12th Sunday in Ordinary Time
    June 25, 2006 93
13th Sunday in Ordinary Time
    July 2, 2006 97
14th Sunday in Ordinary Time
    July 9, 2006 100
15th Sunday in Ordinary Time
    July 16, 2006 102
16th Sunday in Ordinary Time
    July 23, 2006 105
17th Sunday in Ordinary Time
    July 30, 2006 108
Transfiguration
    August 6, 2006 111
18th Sunday in Ordinary Time
    August, 2006 114
19th Sunday in Ordinary Time
    August 13, 2006 117
Vigil of the Feast of the Assumption
    August 14, 2006 120
Feast of the Assumption
    August 15, 2006 122
20th Sunday in Ordinary Time
    August 20, 2006 125
21st Sunday in Ordinary Time
    August 27, 2006 128

22nd Sunday in Ordinary Time
    September 3, 2006 130
23rd Sunday in Ordinary Time
    September 10, 2006 132
24th Sunday in Ordinary Time
    September 17, 2006 135
25th Sunday in Ordinary Time
    September 24, 2006 139
26th Sunday in Ordinary Time
    October 1, 2006 142
27th Sunday in Ordinary Time
    October 8, 2006 145
28th Sunday in Ordinary Time
    October 15, 2006 151
29th Sunday in Ordinary Time
    October 22, 2006 154
30th Sunday in Ordinary Time
    October 29, 2006 157
All Saint
    November 1, 2006 160
31st Sunday in Ordinary Time
    November 5, 2006 163
32nd Sunday in Ordinary Time
    November 12, 2006 166
33rd Sunday in Ordinary Time
    November 19, 2006 169
Thanksgiving
    November 23, 2006 172
Feast of Christ the King
    November 26, 2006 174
Pictures of Rev. Joseph Robinson 177
Shepherds of Christ Prayers 186

Foreward

For years all of us have gone to St. Boniface Church in Cincinnati, Ohio. Our family first lived in this parish – Some of the streets named after our relatives –

Fr. Carter was the founder of the Shepherds of Christ Movement and I, Rita Ring, co-founder –

But my brother, Fr. Joseph Robinson was an important part of my life and our lives as we went to his most holy Masses and listened to his homilies as we formed more and more as a body of people producing the Priestly Newsletter and beginning prayer chapters.

God blessed me and all of us being able to go to his Masses and listen to his homilies –

It is a tremendous honor Fr. Joe has allowed us to share these great gifts with you – for greater holiness and knowing more and more about God –

This is the first of a series of these books – dedicated to our priests, out of love for our beloved Church and all the souls of the world.

As you use these great teachings of homilies Sunday after Sunday – please pray the prayers with us as a network of prayer – praying for the priests, the Church and the world –

I thank God every day for the gift of my older brother who has been an important instrument in his priesthood in my life and the lives of all who went to St. Boniface for Mass.

Rita Ring
Co-founder, Shepherds of Christ Movement

1st Sunday of Advent
November 27, 2005

INTRODUCTION – (Isaiah 63, 16b–17. 19b; 64, 2–7) Today's first reading is a desperate prayer for God to come to save his people. It is one of the most sublime prayers we find in Scripture. God's people were suffering and they knew it was because of their pride and rebellion against their God. They ask for his help and forgiveness. It's a good prayer for us as we begin Advent. We ask God to open our hearts to his coming.

HOMILY – (Mark 13, 33–37) You may have seen the sign "Jesus is coming. Look busy!" As we've heard so many times, the word "advent" means "coming" and the season of advent is a time to prepare for Christ's coming. Jesus tells us emphatically to be alert for that coming. Too often we get overly involved in preparing to celebrate his coming in the past. Of course we are joyful that God has come to us as a little baby 2000 years ago, and it is appropriate that we prepare to celebrate such an awesome event. But that's not all there is to advent and it's not that coming that Jesus is referring to in today's gospel when he tells us to be watchful and to be alert.

Advent is as much about the future as it is about the past. If we do not prepare for his future coming, his coming in the past will be of little value to us. The time for that future coming is unknown to any of us. There will be a time when he comes to each of us personally at the end of our life. None of us are going to be here forever. There will be a time when he comes at the end of the world. If we're prepared for his coming at the end of our lives, we'll be prepared for his other coming in glory at the end of time. Since we do not know when either of those future comings will be, we are inclined to busy ourselves with more pressing things, with more immediate wants and needs.

A few years ago I attended a time management workshop. One of the most useful insights I got out of the workshop is to make a distinction between what is urgent and what is important. They're not always the same thing. For example, a friend calls this afternoon and invites us to a lecture on the sex life of the mosquito. It's urgent. It has to be done right now if we're going to do it. It may not be very important to us unless we're a biologist. Making a will is something important, but it may not be urgent (unless we're on our deathbed). What is important will eventually become urgent, but what is urgent is not always important. I stress this because there are so many things that we feel are urgent at this time of the year. Buy this, send this card, get ready for this event… Some of the urgent things we feel at this time might be important, but we have to be careful not to let them override the most important thing of all: preparing for Christ's coming – an event that we often do not feel so urgent about!

With all the stuff that happens at this time of the year and the stuff we feel we must have, we cannot forget that the child whose birth we celebrate was born in poverty, lived in poverty, died in poverty and taught us not to make "things" too important in our lives. I'm not encouraging poverty, but sometimes we have to work hard not to equate Christmas with a lot of stuff.

Don't think I'm too much of a Scrooge! I enjoy the lights and the music of Christmas. We even have a special Christmas music program here on the 9th of December. I enjoy poinsettias and wreaths and giving and receiving gifts and I enjoy parties. But it's my responsibility to remind myself, and you as well, that this time of the year is first of all meant to enrich us spiritually. If all it does is wear us out and empty our wallets, we've missed the point. Be awake and aware. We are to prepare our hearts to become more the kind of person we know Christ wants us to be. We have Mass every morning, we have two holy hours during the week. After Mass each morning we have either morning prayer in the rectory or rosary in church. We will have a communal penance service in about a week. Even if you can get to church for some extra prayers, I would recommend taking quiet time each day. Quiet time helps us keep things in perspective and it is more important now than at any other time during the year. Our Catholic Update inserted in today's bulletin lists the Scripture readings for each day and a brief reflection. You might also consider putting someone on your gift list who cannot do anything for you in return.

Our Advent wreath reminds us not only how fast the weeks are going before Christmas, but it also reminds us how fast time goes in general. And it reminds us that with each passing week, Christ's light should shine more brightly in our lives. In other centuries Advent had a penitential character and was marked by long fasts. We see remnants of this penitential aspect in the violet vestments and no flowers at the altar and the elimination of the Gloria. It gives a hint that a little self-denial might help us celebrate Christmas with greater joy.

We might ask ourselves as we begin a new Church year, are we any better prepared to meet him today than we were a year ago? If we have backtracked or just stayed in the same place spiritually, we need to hear Jesus once again tells us "stay awake, be alert."

2nd Sunday of Advent
December 4, 2005

INTRODUCTION – (Isaiah 40, 1–5. 9–11; II Peter 3, 8–14; Mark 1, 1–8) Our first reading today introduces that part of Isaiah known as the "Book of Consolation." It is a beautifully comforting message for God's people. For 50 years the Jews had been a captured and enslaved people in Babylon (Iraq today). Now God is about to set them free and allow them to return to their homeland. We'll hear the words "the way of the Lord" frequently in today's readings. It refers to the route by which the Lord would lead his people home. It would be a passage through mountains and desert, a passage that most likely passed through the modern day countries of Iraq and Syria and Lebanon. Isaiah announces this return by calling the people to prepare. Over five hundred years later, John the Baptist would use the same words to call the people of his own day to prepare for the Messiah. Today, Advent calls us to prepare not only for Christmas but also for the day when Christ will call us to leave this world and to be part of his eternal kingdom.

HOMILY – Recently I read a letter from a pastor who said that while he was in the seminary, he taught a class on the history of the Old Testament to prisoners. One evening while he was waiting for a prison guard to come and check him in, he noticed a man waiting in line ahead of him who was fidgeting and constantly checking his watch. The young seminary student thought that man needed a tranquilizer. Finally the guard came. The man hastily scribbled his name in the visitors' book and rushed inside. What does that man do, the seminary student asked. The guard answered: "he teaches a course on serenity through meditation."

The story struck me as an image of many of us at this time of the year. We sing of silent night, peace on earth, joy to the world. At the same time we rush around frantically, doing ten things at once while we're mentally trying to figure out how we're going to do the next ten things on our list!

Last week our Lord told us to be watchful, to be alert, to be ready for his coming, not his coming as a baby, but his coming in glory at the end. After I made some suggestions last week of some spiritual things people might do during Advent, I thought perhaps I would see lot of new faces at morning Mass or Holy Hour! But that was not the case. I know not everyone can get to Mass or Holy Hour, but hopefully more people are spending some extra quiet time at home reading the scriptures or praying or maybe more people are doing some extra good works.

Today the scriptures give us a similar message: "prepare." We all know we won't be ready for anything important unless we prepare. Maybe we're already ready to meet our Maker, I hope I am and I hope you are too, but maybe there's a little room for improvement in a few of us.

One of the cartoons this week was very clever. Garfield the cat was listening to a Christmas carol and as he listened he said: "Ah, the first Christmas carol of the season. It hard to believe that in just three short weeks I'm gonna be sick of that sucker." We don't like to wait. We want to get to Christmas without having to wait.

But Advent is a time of waiting. It's not passive waiting like when we were students in school and we kept looking at the clock waiting for the school bell to ring. It's active waiting, like a recently married husband

and wife expecting the birth of their first child, trying to get ready for the great event. St. Peter reminds us everything we know will disappear for us some day and since that is going to happen, "what sort of persons ought you to be?" Paul asks. He answers his own question: we should be the sort of person who conducts ourselves "in holiness and devotion..."

Christmas is a day we must prepare for in a spiritual manner if we want to experience the spiritual joy of God's great love and be more ready to welcome his future coming. Otherwise when Christmas day ends we'll be saying to ourselves: "Boy, am I glad that's over." Christmas will be for any of us only what we make of it. Amen.

Feast of the Immaculate Conception
December 8, 2005

(Gen. 3, 9–15, 20; Luke 1, 26–38) The feast today is about Mary's conception, that from the instant she began to exist on this earth, indeed from her very conception, she was holy, filled with God's grace and without sin. The gospel today can confuse us somewhat because it tells us about Jesus' conception. It was read today, first of all, because there is no gospel telling us about the moment when Mary was conceived. And secondly today's gospel does give us an important piece of information about Mary related to today's feast. The angel greeted her as: "Full of grace." Our feast celebrates what the angel stated. There was no moment in Mary's life when God's grace did not fill her. She was full of grace.

As we listen in on this conversation between Mary and the Angel, we learn not only about Mary but also about the child she is going to have. Mary's son to be would be Son of the Most High and king forever. Her child will be called "holy, the Son of God." In the midst of all our business, we pause on this Holy Day to think what it is we are happy about at this time of year.

This is why Mary was "full of grace," so she could give birth to the source of all holiness and grace, God's own Son. And why did he come to us? So that we too can become holy. This is what St. Paul tells us in today's second reading: "God chose us in him to be holy and blameless in his sight."

Holiness is something few people strive for. All of us want to get to heaven, but most of us would probably tend to say I just want to get inside the door. We should do more than just try to get inside the door. We are called to be holy. Most of us never think that becoming holy is our vocation. We usually think holiness is for someone else, like the saints or people in religious orders. That's because we do not understand holiness. We think being holy means spending all day praying or wearing ourselves out doing good things for others and never having a chance to have any fun. I think holy people probably have as much fun as any of us, but there's something greater than fun. It is joy and peace and love. To be holy means to be close to God. The closer we are to God, the more we will be filled with love and joy and peace – both in this life and throughout eternity.

Our vocation to holiness is illustrated by the two stories we heard today.

The first story was about our first parents who originally were very close to God and were very happy. That was the symbolism of the Garden of Eden. But that wasn't good enough for them. They wanted to be like

God himself. So they rebelled against God and they lost all they had.

The second story, the annunciation, illustrates Mary's constant attitude of being willing to say "yes" to God. It was only through her openness that the Son of the Most High has come to us. St. Luke tells us Mary was not only holy and always ready to do whatever God wanted of her, but he also tells us she was joyful. Holiness and joy are connected. After the angel left Mary, St. Luke told us about Mary visiting her cousin and she was full of joy. She expressed her joy in the beautiful hymn "the Magnificat." My soul gives glory to the Lord and my spirit rejoices in God my savior."

In reflecting on the holiness of Mary, we may feel as if we were treated unfairly. We were born with original sin. The deck was stacked against us from the beginning. But we forget that when we were baptized we were filled with God's life. The very same grace that filled Mary at the moment of her conception, filled us when we were baptized. So holiness is possible for us too. Our two stories can show us there are two ways each of us can go in life. We can follow the example of our first parents, Adam and Eve, or we can follow the example of Mary. The first will lead to sorrow, the other to joy. To imitate Mary, all we have to do is say "yes" to whatever God asks of us.

3rd Sunday of Advent
December 11, 2005

INTRODUCTION – (Isaiah 61, 1–2a. 10–11; I Thessalonians 5, 16–24; John 1, 6–8. 19–28) As the celebration of Christ's birth draws near, joy is in the air. It's also reflected in today's liturgy. The prophet speaking to us in our first reading tells us he was sent to bring glad tidings to the poor, that he rejoices in the Lord, and in God is the joy of his soul. The response, which is almost always from the Book of Psalms, is today taken from St. Luke's gospel. It is Mary's hymn of joy which she enthusiastically proclaimed when she visited her cousin Elizabeth after the annunciation. St. Paul in the second reading tells us to rejoice always. His instruction "rejoice" implies that rejoicing is more of a choice in attitude rather than a feeling that spontaneously comes over us. John the Baptist, whom we meet in the gospel, was an austere person, but his message was a joyful one, joyful because the Lord was coming. John was honored to have been chosen by God to point him out and to prepare the people for that coming.

HOMILY – John the Baptist announced the coming of the Lord. And I announce to you the coming of Sister Ann who will make an appeal for the Retirement for Religious at the end of Mass. So I will try to keep my remarks brief.

Recently I read a book about Mother Theresa and in the spirit of today's liturgy, a spirit of joy, I would like to make a couple of comments about her. She was once asked if she ever got discouraged. She answered that she is always happy. "Discouragement comes from pride," she always said. "We must be people of hope. It's not success that matters to God but faithfulness. Never stop trying."

You can imagine she had a lot of problems and cares in her ministry, yet she did not worry about yesterday or tomorrow. She often said, "Do what you can, do it now and do it well." People of all walks of life, of every social standing and position went to her. She always gave them what she referred to as her business card. It was one of the most profound, yet simple, statements of the spiritual life I have ever come across. It said: "The fruit of silence is prayer. The fruit of prayer is faith. The fruit of faith is love. The fruit of love is service. And the fruit of service is peace." Have you got my business card she would ask. First of all she gave God her time, then she gave people her time, her faith and her tender charity and all went away from her with hope.

In a letter she wrote to a member of her community, we hear echoes of St. Paul who told us in today's second reading, "Rejoice always." She wrote, "Do not be afraid, Jesus said. Put your hand in his hand and walk with him all the way. Keep the joy of loving Jesus in your heart, and share this joy with all you meet." Amen.

Fourth Sunday of Advent
December 18, 2005

INTRODUCTION – (2 Samuel 7,1–5, 8b–12, 14a,16; Luke 1, 26–38) Our first reading goes back 1000 years before Christ to the time of king David in Jerusalem. You need to recall that when Moses led the people of Israel out of Egypt, almost 300 years before King David, God gave the people a special sign of his presence among them. That sign was the Arc of the Covenant. It looked something like this: a box in which were placed the 10 Commandments, a lid of gold and on the lid were two angels. The box was carried by two long poles because no one could touch the Arc. The two angels provided a throne for their invisible God, Yahweh. As Moses and the people moved through the desert and eventually into the promised land, the Arc was kept in a tent. Only designated people, and eventually only the high priest, could enter the tent and offer sacrifice to God. The Arc was still kept in a tent during the reign of King David. David had built himself a nice comfortable palace and he decided it was not right that the Arc, the special sign of God's presence with his people, was still kept in a tent. So he told his prophet, Nathan, that he would build a temple, a house for God. Nathan said "good idea," but God said "no." God said David had shed too much blood in his role as king, so he would have David's son, Solomon, build the temple after David died. But God was pleased with David's idea and blessed him. One of the special blessings David received was that David's line would never die out. One of his descendants would always be king over God's people. That's what is meant by the statement that God would "establish a house" for David. For about 400 years this proved to be true. Always the king of Judea was of the royal house of David. When the Babylonians conquered the Jews, that was the end of the kingship. But the Jews never forgot the promise God made to David and always waited for one who would come from David's family who would rescue God's people from their enemies and restore the kingdom to Israel. Since kings were anointed when they assumed power, the king they looked for was called the anointed one – the Hebrew word for "anointed one" is Messiah, in Greek the word is Christos. In the gospel of the annunciation, the angel Gabriel informs Mary that her son would be the fulfillment of these hopes. "The Lord God will give him the throne of David his father, and he will rule over the house of Jacob forever, and of his kingdom there will be no end."

HOMILY – The angel Gabriel announced the birth of a king: "the Lord God will give him the throne of David, his father, and he will rule over the house of Jacob forever, and of his kingdom there will be no end." I love the interesting way St. Luke begins to tell us about this. He first of all introduces Mary, but not in the usual way we introduce someone. We would have said, "I would like you to meet Mary. She's from Galilee and engaged to be married to Joseph." None of us would have dared to add to our introduction: "She's a virgin!" But it's a very important thing St. Luke wants us to know and he tells us she's a virgin even before he tells us Mary's name. Why? Because Mary would conceive in a miraculous way, through the power of the Holy Spirit. That alone was spectacular, but that was only the beginning of the most unique and wonderful event this world would ever see. This king, who would be conceived by the power of the Holy Spirit, would be more than the ordinary, run of the mill king. This king, the messiah, the christos; that is, the anointed one, would be king over a kingdom that would never end. To top that, because he was conceived by God's own Spirit, he would be the "Son of God."

This is an awesome mystery that God took on our human flesh and became like us in every way except sin. There is a special theological term for it: the Incarnation. The God, who dwelt among his people housed in a tent for many generations, now comes to live with his people as one of us, taking on our own flesh and blood. Sometimes people like to say Jesus was a great prophet or a great teacher or a great humanitarian but that's all he was. The gospels tell us he is the Son of God. If he was less than that, there was nothing great about him because he was a crazy man, full of delusion and paranoia. There is no in-between position we can take on Jesus. [In today's bulletin is a copy of the Catholic Update that gives a beautiful explanation of today's gospel. I highly recommend it.]

How we live our faith depends on how firmly we believe in this wonderful event. If we truly believe God has come into our world and into our lives through Jesus, shouldn't we try to spend time with him, shouldn't we try to get to know him better and follow him as well as possible? If we are not ready to do that, could it be that our faith is little more than a lot of words?

One last thought. I would like you to notice the respect God showed Mary in the annunciation. God didn't just tell her she would be the mother of such an awesome person. God asked her if she would be and waited for her answer. We have here a cue for how the Son of God can come to us more fully. We have here a cue for how Christmas can fully fill our hearts. We have here a cue for how to enjoy the blessings of his kingdom that will have no end. God's Son wants to live in each of us. As God did with Mary, God waits for each of us to answer him as to whether he is welcome. Are we able to say as Mary did: "I am the servant of the Lord. I will do whatever you want of me, Oh God."

Christmas
December 25, 2005

We just heard the story of Jesus' birth. We've heard it over and over, yet our hearts rejoice to hear it again. Our God came to us, not in majesty and glory, blinding us with his brilliance and deafening us with the sound of his voice. Our God came to us in humility and poverty and simplicity. He showed us, by sharing in our life, that there is goodness in the world he created, goodness in the life he gave us, goodness in all of us and that we are worth saving, even worth dying for. Words alone cannot express the wonders we celebrate today. And so we express our words in song. No celebration throughout the year has so many songs dedicated to it. It is a time for singing. But to celebrate today's feast, even singing is inadequate. We put up statues picturing Jesus' birth. They help us understand more fully God's humble coming to us. We thank St. Francis for that. He tried to think of a special way to celebrate God's love, a way that even the youngest child could understand. So, one day he asked one of his friends to prepare a cave with a manger filled with straw and animals in the cave. There were no statues there, not even a statue of baby Jesus. It was just a stable with live animals, an ox, a donkey and sheep, similar to the stable of Bethlehem where Jesus was born. He placed an altar over the manger, so people would make the connection in their minds that just as Jesus came to us as a human, he comes to us today as our food and our drink. St. Francis was a deacon. When Mass was celebrated at midnight that year, he read the gospel and preached of God's love and Jesus' birth. Some people even saw the baby Jesus lying in the crib and they saw Francis pick up the baby and hold it. Francis, who also gave us the stations of the cross, has helped to bring Christmas alive for all of us through the Christmas crib.

I always look for a story to help us see in a new way what Christmas is all about. This is a story by a writer named Barbara Baumgardner. Barbara's husband died and her first Christmas without him was not joyful. It was very painful for her. During the following year her pain in losing her husband began to heal and the second Christmas after he died, she began to get excited that Christmas was coming and she decided to celebrate it with her two daughters. They both lived out of town but she invited them to her home for a big Christmas dinner. She had decorated everything in sight, baked lots of goodies and had Christmas music playing on the CD. Her house looked, smelled and sounded like Christmas. Three days before Christmas her first daughter called and had frozen water pipes at home and couldn't come. She had to take care of the mess the frozen pipes caused. Within twenty minutes Barbara's second daughter, who lived on a farm, called and said in her area the wind chill factor was 45 below zero and they had farm animals which she had to care for, so she couldn't come. Barbara would have gone to visit her daughter in a minute, but Barbara was stuck at home. She had already invited a few neighbors to join her family on Christmas. Her brother-in-law, who was recently widowed, along with his 84 year old mother was coming, and a young single man from church, and the widow next door who had just gotten out of the hospital, and she had promised to bring a plate of food to the old man across the street. She didn't invite him because he was always so filthy and smelled like stale cigars. She was going to let everyone join her family dinner on Christmas and now there was no family. She suddenly felt very much alone and was feeling very sorry for herself. She complained to God that he was not fair. Her family wasn't coming and she was stuck having to entertain all those other people. She kept asking God why he let her invite all those other people when he knew her family wouldn't be able to be with her on Christmas. In the silence of her misery she began to hear God answer her complaints. God said, "I know it's Christmas, Barbara; it's my birthday. What did you get me?" "What, God, what do you mean?" she asked. "Whose birthday is it?" he insisted. "What did you get me?" Well, Barbara started thinking "What can I get you, Lord? Maybe I can be nicer to my neighbor, maybe instead of just taking food to that smelly old man across the street, I can invite him and his dog to come and have dinner with us. It would blow his mind! Maybe I can invite someone from the homeless shelter and the checker at the grocery store who will probably be alone on Christmas." Before long she said her party was full, but not as full as her heart. She said she did not remember having so much fun on Christmas as the day she gave her Christmas to Jesus as a birthday gift.

Many people today want to take Christ out of Christmas and just celebrate for some other reason. That's their loss. The heart of our celebration is God's love shown to us in Jesus Christ. We are grateful to the gospel writers for telling us about that blessed event. We are grateful to St. Francis for helping to make it more concrete for us through the crib. We are grateful for the composers of music who have helped us put our joy into song. We are grateful to all of you who have come to make this a special celebration today. Amen.

Mary Mother of God
January 1, 2006

(Numbers 6: 22-27; Galatians 4: 4-7; Luke 2: 16-21) In an article written by Billy Graham he reflected on the year 1809. In that year all of Europe was preoccupied with the Napoleonic Wars. No one was thinking about babies. The world was not thinking of Alfred Lord Tennyson, Oliver Wendell Holmes, Felix Mendelssohn or Abraham Lincoln who were born that same year. In 1809 in the ashes of war and destruction, seeds of hope and new life were already starting to grow. The story is told that the day Abraham Lincoln was born in Kentucky, one of the villagers was asked what was happening in the village. The reply was, "Nothing at all, nothing at all – except a new baby born at Tom Lincoln's house. Nothing ever happens out here."

Today we are preoccupied with the war with Iraq, threats of terrorism, threats of nuclear proliferation, worries about the economy, abortions, poverty and family problems, you name it. But somewhere seeds of hope and new life are starting to sprout. The shepherds in Bethlehem 2000 years ago saw a baby boy in a manger and recognized in him new hope. We are in the midst of celebrating the greatest hope we have, the mystery of God taking on our human flesh. The mystery of Christmas is too much for any of us to absorb in one day or even in one century. And so we celebrate it again today with the feast of Mary, the Mother of God. This, the first and oldest feast of Mary in the Church, honors Mary and it reminds us again of the mystery of the Incarnation, that God took on our human flesh, without ceasing to be God. Although there are two natures in Jesus Christ, human and divine, there is only one person, the Second Person of the Blessed Trinity, and Mary is his mother. Thus she is rightly called: "Mother of God." Perhaps when all nations finally comprehend the depth of this mystery, then we will know true peace.

We must deal with current problems, but we cannot give up hope. The birth of Jesus assures us that God did not give up on us but rather came down to us to enable us to someday live with him. And he offers us the help we need each day. Christ told us "I came that they might have life and might have it to the full." The fullness of life is something that is still ahead, a life we hope to share with the Lord for all eternity. If we didn't have that to look forward to we could easily be overwhelmed by the problems of life. Jesus ended his Sermon on the Mount with that image: "Everyone who listens to these words of mine and acts on them will be like a wise person who built his house on rock. The rain fell, the floods came, and the winds blew and buffeted the house. But it did not collapse; it had been set solidly on rock. And everyone who listens to these words of mine but does not act on them will be like a fool who built his house on sand. The rain fell, the floods came, and the winds blew and buffeted the house. And it collapsed and was completely ruined."

I cannot end my homily today without some reference to time. It does not stop. I'm sure most of us have expressed the sentiment in the past few weeks: "I can't believe it's December already," or "I can't believe we're already celebrating Christmas." Time keeps moving. "Tomorrow and tomorrow and tomorrow creeps in this petty pace from day to day..." as Macbeth says, and it keeps on creeping. And none of us knows when time will run out for us. Many people make resolutions today because they recognize there are some things they would like to do differently (like spend less money, stop smoking, lose weight, exercise more, etc.) and they know they don't have forever to get around to doing it. If you're making any resolutions, why not think about praying a little more. Whenever I pray, I am tempted to think I'm giving some of my precious time to God. Then God reminds me every moment I am alive, he is giving to me. When I pray, I am only giving back to God what is already his. Prayer helps keep me sane and helps me keep things in perspective. Wouldn't 15 minutes of prayer each day be more benefit to us than 15 minutes of TV? We have the example of Mary in today's gospel. "Mary kept all these things and reflected on them in her heart." She who was already so close to God <u>needed</u> time to reflect on the presence of God in her life....... Is this need any less for any of us?

Feast of the Epiphany
January 8, 2006

INTRODUCTION – (Isaiah 60,1-6; Mt. 2,1-12) God's people were conquered and enslaved by the Babylonians in 587 B.C. Fifty years later the Persians conquered the Babylonians and they allowed the Jews to return home. As our first reading begins, we hear the prophet enthusiastically proclaim this return: "Rise up in splendor, Jerusalem! Your light has come..." The prophet, however, sees in this event something much grander than the Jews' return from captivity. He sees Jerusalem becoming the center of spirituality and light for all the world. This passage begins to see its fulfillment in Jesus' death and resurrection in Jerusalem. From there his light spreads out to all the world. Unfortunately, not all people choose to follow this light, but at the end of time, those who have followed Christ's light will enter into the new and eternal Jerusalem so beautifully described in the book of Revelation.

HOMILY – I have a postcard from one of my vacations in Florida. It is a picture of the ocean with sand dunes, sea gulls, waves breaking on the beach, sea oats, etc. I pull it out and look at it when I'm feeling especially stressed. The picture reminds me of peaceful times I've had and restful vacations I can still look forward to. As you think of that image, keep in mind that it is a picture of one tiny portion of an immense body of water.

Now I want to use this as an example of an experience of God. I'm sure we've all had many of them. Perhaps in prayer, perhaps at Mass or in reading the Scriptures, perhaps in nature, perhaps in childbirth, perhaps in a loving and kind person, perhaps even in suffering. These experiences are moments to treasure. They could be called "epiphanies" for us for the word "epiphany" means God manifesting himself to us. Like the ocean God is vast, eternal, all powerful, all wise, all loving, greater than the universe. Those little epiphanies any of us may have had are just one very tiny experience of the infinite God.

Today we hear about the epiphany of three magi. This word magi comes from the original Greek text which calls them "magoi." Most likely they were from Persia or Babylon, and were priests of the Zoroastrian religion, known for their wisdom and their ability to interpret dreams and astrological phenomena. The gospels do not tell us how many there were. The idea of their being three of them comes from the three gifts they offered. The idea that they were kings did not originate until the third century, primarily inspired by Psalm 72 in which we prayed: "the kings of Tarshish and the Isles shall offer gifts, the kings of Arabia and Seba shall bring tribute. All kings shall pay him homage..." King Herod obviously was not one of those kings who would pay Jesus homage.

Nature and Scripture led them to the infant Jesus. But in finding him they evidently knew they had found something far greater than just another child. The magi disappear from the Scriptures and from history, but the revelation of God's Son to us, in other words, Epiphany, is not finished with their disappearance. There was his baptism in the Jordan and Jesus' first miracle at the wedding feast of Cana, for example, which were at one time celebrated as part of this feast. All of Jesus' miracles were manifestations of his divine power, including and especially the resurrection.

Epiphanies are all around us if we are alert to them. When we have experiences of God's love and presence, personal epiphanies, they convince us there is a God. But too many people do not move any further in their knowledge and experience of God. They are content with their own personal epiphany and they miss the spiritual growth that comes from diligently searching further for him. There is no spiritual growth for them. Let us return to the analogy of sitting on the beach in Florida. It's enjoyable to sit there and watch the waves, but takes no effort on our part. To really appreciate the ocean we have to know what many other people have learned in their own travels. The ocean is as much off the coast of Maine as off the coast of South Africa. If we want to know God, we need more than just a couple of experiences of God's love and presence. This is why we need religion and we need the Church. People say they don't need organized religion. They don't realize how practical and helpful it truly is. By limiting our knowledge of the ocean to one tiny location we'll never get anywhere else or be very safe if we try. If we are to grow and mature in our relationship with God, we need information, especially maps, from others if we want to go somewhere further. We need the experience and guidance of other spiritual persons who can teach us what we do not yet know.

Epiphanies are wonderful. We should take and treasure all those that come our way. But they are meant to be helps along the journey we are all called to make to come to know and to possess the greatest treasure life can offer us in this world or the next, Jesus Christ, whom we can never get enough of. Amen.

2nd Sunday in Ordinary Time
January 15, 2006

(I Sam. 3,3b-10.19; Jn. 1,35-42) Once while I was at another parish I went to visit a lady in the hospital. She was the mother of a large number of children (more than ten), several of them still in grade school. In our visit she disclosed to me that she thought she had a vocation to be a nun. It was both humorous and sad, sad that she was so seriously detached from real life and humorous because with all those children underfoot, I could see why she wanted to get away from it all.

My point is that not every time we think we're getting a call from God is it really God calling us. Often when he really does call us, his call is not so easy to discern, or if we discern where it's coming from, we're not so quick to follow. For example, Moses was in no hurry to take on the job God was asking him to do, even though the message came with unmistakable clarity. Samuel, on the other hand, kept hearing God call, but didn't know it was God. It was his mentor, the high priest, Eli, who helped him know God's voice. When I felt God calling me to be a priest, I was excited about the idea until I reached puberty. Then I was hoping the idea would go away, but God kept calling like he did with Samuel. The call to the apostles seems to have taken place over the course of time, as they found themselves attracted by Jesus' powerful personality. We see in today's gospel that God's call does not always come out of the heavens but from another human being. The call to Andrew and an unnamed apostle (probably John) came from John the Baptist. Peter's call started with Andrew. It took a while after meeting Jesus before they gave up their lucrative business in order to be Jesus' disciple or as that word means, Jesus' student.

When God's calls, we seldom know what we are getting ourselves into if we follow that call. Samuel didn't know that he would become a leader for God's people, that he would be a prophet and priest, that he would lead the Israelites into battle, and that he would raise up and depose kings. Mary, the mother of Jesus, didn't know what she was in for when she said "yes" to God. Nor did the apostles know that they would have to give up more than their fishing business, and that following Jesus would cost them their lives. Mother Teresa felt called to be a nun and started her vocation in the classroom. After almost 20 years of teaching she received what she described as a "call within the call" when she felt called to serve the poorest of the poor and start a new religious order. Martin Luther King could not have had any idea when he was in the seminary and getting "C's" in public speaking that he would be threatened daily, that he would be imprisoned for standing up for justice, that he would be facing angry crowds with equanimity and prayer for his persecutors, that he would one day be leading 200,000 people to the nation's capital to dramatize that all of America's citizens are endowed with certain unalienable rights, among which are life, liberty and the pursuit of happiness. Nor did he know that an assassin's bullet would end his life at age 39. If I had known when I entered the seminary some of the difficulties I would have to deal with as a priest, I would have said, "God, I can't do that. Find someone else." I'm glad I didn't know, I'm glad God was with me during hard times, and I'm glad I followed his call.

God's call sometimes disrupts our comfortable lives. But if God wants us he'll keep calling, like he did Samuel, as long as there's a chance we might respond. Sometimes we need help in knowing what God's saying, sometimes we need to be pointed in the right direction, sometimes we need confirmation from others. For example, when I went to the seminary, the rector and staff didn't assume that I really had a calling. We had to go through nine years of schooling and a lot of scrutiny before ordination. When the lady in the hospital with all the kids told me she felt called to be a nun, I couldn't support her. Instead I reminded her that her real vocation was to take care of her children.

I think it's extremely important to notice that Samuel was already in God's presence at the place where the Arc of the Covenant was being kept, and it was in the quiet of the night he heard the Lord. Almost every time I have heard the Lord speaking to me, it was when I was praying, reading the Scriptures or meditating.

Our environment calls to us from so many directions: TV, radio, e-mail, cell phones, beepers, billboards, etc., etc. A lot of times God gets put on hold so we can listen to a call from somewhere else. If we want to hear the Lord, we have to put all other voices on hold so God can get through. The only way we can do that is to set time aside. I have a phrase I use for myself all the time regarding prayer: "if you don't schedule it in, you schedule it out." We have to make time for the Lord if we're really going to hear him, and if we don't, we won't. Amen.

3rd Sunday in Ordinary Time
January 22, 2006

INTRODUCTION – (Jonah 3,1-5.10; Mk. 1,14-20) Whenever we think of Jonah we think of his being swallowed whole by a great fish (the Bible makes no mention of a whale). The story of how he was swallowed by a fish is a long one, but basically he was trying to escape from the mission God gave him to preach repentance to the Assyrians. You need to know that the Assyrians were an especially warlike, aggressive, merciless people who lived on the Tigris River, 250 miles north of Baghdad. The Assyrians had already destroyed most of Israel by the time Jonah was written, so you can imagine there was deep hatred on the part of the Jews for the Assyrians. Jonah was three days in the belly of the fish before he was spit out on the shore of Assyria. Having learned he couldn't run away from God, Jonah decided he had better do what God wanted. The story about Jonah that we hear in our first reading today is more amazing than the part of the story about the fish. Without miracles or spectacular signs, Jonah preached a one line, unenthusiastic warning to the people of Nineveh and in one day converted the entire city of Nineveh. To get an idea of how astonishing this would be, think of an unknown individual showing up in Baghdad today and in one day every person, including all the terrorists, repenting and converting to Christianity. Would that be something or what!!! Today's reading shows God is not interested in punishing people but in giving all people, even the bad guys, a chance to reform. The passage sets the theme for the gospel when Jesus began his public ministry by preaching repentance. We know from real life experience and from the experience Jesus and the Apostles had, calling people to change their lives is not as easy as the story of Jonah makes it appear to be.

HOMILY – This week the mayor of New Orleans, acting like an Old Testament prophet, said (and I quote): "Surely God is mad at America. He sent us hurricane after hurricane after hurricane, and it's

destroyed and put stress on this country." He added: "…
surely he (God) is upset at black America also."
Whenever something bad happens many people, like a
knee jerk reaction, like to say "God must be punishing
us." If the mayor of New Orleans had received a true
anointing to be God's prophet, he would have warned
people ahead of time and not just after the fact. The
picture of God that the mayor of New Orleans paints, as
an angry God punishing us because we've been bad, is
not the picture of the God I know. Even God in the Old
Testament often pictured as a God of wrath, is
interested in saving people, not in destroying them; for
example, in our first reading God sent Jonah to warn the
cruel and warlike people of Nineveh so they would not
be destroyed. Why are there hurricanes and natural
disasters? I think it's just part of living on a planet that
is constantly adjusting to natural forces. And maybe we
are making things worse by the way we abuse our
environment. However, there are times when bad things
do happen because we do not do what God wants. We
have a God who wants only good things for us and for
that reason he tells us how we should live in order to
guide us to what is best for us. And when we ignore him,
we only cause problems for ourselves.

This is why God sent his Son to us, to teach us and
guide us. "The time has come," he said as he began his
public ministry. "The Kingdom of God is near. Turn
away from your sins and believe in this good news." As
we heard in today's gospel, Jesus needed help to
announce this good news so he started choosing people
who would help him.

Jesus said "I came that they may have life and may
have it to the full." Jesus' teachings are good news.
Sometimes, though, it doesn't feel that way. Forgiving
people who have hurt us, loving our enemies, getting up

on Sunday morning when we're tired, keeping the commandments, giving some of our hard earned money to others; sometimes it doesn't feel like good news. That's why he said, "believe in this good news," because we don't always feel it.

Turn away from sin is part of his message. "Turn away from sin" is the translation of a word from the Greek: μετάνοια which means a change of mind. Generally it is translated repentance or conversion. Jesus is telling us if we're going to start believing in what he tells us we have to change our mind, to stop thinking and believing and doing what we used to.

Of course the reason we are here is because we do believe in Christ. But unless there's a Mother Theresa among us, I suspect there is room for improvement in most of us. Jesus' call to conversion is sort of like New Year's resolutions. We make New Year's resolutions because we realize we can do better, we can be better, we have more potential than we are using.

Until we hopefully reach heaven where we will be perfect, there'll always be room for improvement, always be some areas of our lives where the gospel of Jesus has not yet penetrated. Would that conversion were as easy as the book of Jonah pictures it. If it were, we wouldn't have to be reminded of it so often. Amen.

4th Sunday in Ordinary Time
January 29, 2006

INTRODUCTION – (Deut 18, 15-20; I Cor. 7, 32-35; Mark 1, 21-28) I would like to begin by saying something about our second reading. It needs a special explanation. We have to understand when we hear Paul that he was thinking Jesus was going to return soon, that "time is short" and "the world as we know it is passing away." From this perspective, he favors a celibate life style. As a celibate himself he sees its advantages, but he admits not everyone is called to that kind of life. I think he overemphasizes the advantages of celibacy. He argues that married people do not have as much commitment to the Lord as those who are celibate, which may or may not be true. For a marriage to work, one of the things married couples need is a strong commitment to the Lord. And I can only partly agree with Paul when he suggests celibacy leaves a person free of anxiety. Maybe not being married saves a priest from certain forms of anxiety, but there are enough other anxieties connected with celibacy and the priesthood.

Now about today's first reading: Moses led God's people from slavery in Egypt. Moses remained with God's people in the desert for a generation before they were ready to enter the Promised Land. Moses himself knew he would die before the people crossed the Jordan to enter the land. In today's first reading Moses is speaking to God's people shortly before he dies. He assures them God would not leave them without direction or leadership. God would send them another prophet like himself who would speak God's word to them. This reading prepares us for the gospel where Jesus speaks God's word with power and authority.

HOMILY – St. Mark's gospel is the shortest of the gospels and St. Mark doesn't spend any time with preliminaries. He opens his gospel with a few words about John the Baptist, then he tells us briefly about Jesus' baptism and his fasting and temptation in the desert. Last week we heard about Jesus beginning to gather his apostles and today we hear Jesus is already busy teaching and healing. And we're only at verse 21 in Mark's first chapter. St. Mark even skips past whatever it was Jesus was preaching about to get right to where the action is. Jesus comes out on the offensive, attacking the powers of evil. Notice it was on the Sabbath, the day the Jews celebrated God delivering his people from slavery. So it's appropriate that on this particular Sabbath, the man in the gospel was set free from slavery to the devil.

I have prayed many times over people who felt the devil had some power over them. I've never had such a dramatic experience as St. Mark describes here (people convulsing, crying out, sometimes falling down). I have read about people who have. The movie *The Exorcist,* which many people may have seen, was based on a true story of an exorcism. It's interesting how popular angels are right now and how unpopular it is to believe in the devil. It's especially interesting that so many people have this attitude when there is so much evil in the world around us. Personally I believe in good angels, but I find it much easier to believe in the bad ones. I think there's so much more evidence of their existence. Our ignoring the presence of the devil gives the devil greater freedom to do his or her thing. The smartest strategy a devil can use is to convince us that he or she is not around. St. Peter tells us "your enemy, the devil, roams around like a roaring lion, looking for someone to devour. Be firm in your faith and resist him." (1 Peter 5, 8-9) Although some instances of what was considered demon possession at the time of Jesus may have been psychological or physical (such as epilepsy), the gospels do take the devil seriously and Jesus did too. When I am asked to pray over someone who thinks they are under demonic power, I always try to rule out psychological problems. If I think it is warranted, I do suggest a psychologist or psychiatrist for them to see, but at times I have felt there was an evil power at work in their lives that went beyond psychology.

Notice the devil recognized Jesus immediately as the Son of God: "the Holy One of God." Devils may not be good but they are very smart. It's not until the end of St. Mark's gospel, as Jesus dies on the cross, that any human person recognizes who Jesus really is. And that person was a pagan, a Roman centurian, who after seeing Jesus die, said: "Truly, this man was the Son of God." It took people a long time to find out who Jesus was, the devil recognized it immediately.

St. Mark tells us when Jesus taught the people and healed the possessed man his audience was spellbound and filled with awe.

The gospels not only tell us about Jesus, they tell us also about ourselves. What is the gospel telling us about ourselves today? It is asking us: how do we react to Jesus? Are we filled with wonder and awe when we hear him or think of him. Aesop told us over 2500 years ago: "Familiarity breeds contempt." Maybe we don't have contempt of our Lord, but after hearing about him for many years, our sense of awe and wonder can get dulled. How do we rekindle that excitement of hearing about him again? One way I know of is not to think we know all there is to know about him. We have to keep discovering more and more about him. Jesus is the infinite Son of God and whatever we know about him is just a tiny little bit compared to what we have yet to discover. We can only do that through prayer. Today we pray the greatest prayer there is, a prayer Jesus himself gave us at the Last Supper. But our prayer life has to include more than just one hour a week in church. It must continue through the week. If Mass is the only prayer we pray all week, the Mass itself will become boring and dry.

Another way to recapture that sense of awe in Jesus is to praise him. Too often our prayers are limited to asking God for things we need or want. And that's good. But praise is also an important part of prayer and praise helps to lift our hearts to a sense of wonder as we come before our God. In Mass today we try to capture that sense of wonder and awe through the selection of hymns of praise. We praise God who has come to teach us and to help us with our everyday struggles with life and with the powers of evil around us.

5th Sunday in Ordinary Time
February 5, 2006

INTRODUCTION – (Job 7, 1-4. 6-7; Mark 1, 29-39) The book of Job was written about 400-500 years before Christ. At that time the Jews did not know about reward and punishment in the next life. In their view, the spirits of the dead simply dwelled in a place called Sheol, where they were neither happy nor unhappy. Yet the Jews believed that God was fair and just and that God rewarded those who were good and punished those who were evil. Having no concept of happiness or unhappiness in the next life, they could only conclude that good people would be rewarded in this life and bad people would be punished. So, they reasoned that if someone was successful and prosperous, they must be good people because God was rewarding them so generously, and if someone was sick or was suffering in some way, they must be bad people even if their evil deeds were known only by God. But their theology was not reality. Good people do suffer and bad people often get by with murder. That is the issue the book of Job tries to deal with. Job is introduced to us as a genuinely good person (God himself says what a good man he is) and initially he is prosperous and successful in every way. But a number of catastrophes come along that destroy his fortune, his family and his health. Today we hear Job at an extremely low point in his life. If you've never known depression, this is a good description of it. Job's lament prepares us for the gospel where we hear about Jesus saving people from sickness and suffering.

HOMILY – Jesus did not invent the idea of healing people miraculously. When I was visiting Greece several years ago, I stopped to visit an ancient shrine to the Greek god, Asclepius, who, in mythology, was the son of Apollo. It was a place of healing, and hanging on the walls of the shrine were little plaster molds of body parts that people believed Asclepius had healed. The Hebrew Scriptures (a.k.a. the Old Testament) tell us of the healing power of the prophets Elijah and Elisha over 800 years before Christ. But there is no person or no movement or no god in any of the ancient writings who is more associated with healing than Jesus Christ. Healing was as much a part of his ministry as teaching. Indeed his healings were a way of teaching. His healings taught about the power of God, the love of God, the power of faith. His healings were concrete, tangible signs of the hidden spiritual healing and life he came to bring us.

Healing did not stop with Jesus. In the Acts of the Apostles we read how his apostles continued his work of healing. You could almost say that Christianity was as much a religion of healing as it was a religion promising us eternal life if we live a good life. About four hundred years after Christ, St. Augustine, the great theologian, claimed that the time for healings had ceased. He said they were needed in the early Church to help the Church grow, but by his time they were not necessary. Shortly before St. Augustine died, he wrote that he had been wrong about that. As bishop he had witnessed many healings in his own diocese and that God continues to cure people through prayer and through the power of the risen Jesus.

From the beginning, the Church has had a sacrament to pray for the sick but in later centuries it was used only to prepare people for death. The sacrament is based on the words of St. James in his epistle - when someone is sick they should call for the priests of the church and be anointed with oil. Gratefully, Vatican II restored it to its original purpose of praying for healing. It is still given when a person is near death because it is also a source of spiritual healing, grace and peace.

The age of miracles was not over at the time of St. Augustine and it is not over today. One proof of that is there must be evidence of true miracles attributed to every person who is canonized. Our late pope, John Paul, canonized a lot of people in his pontificate.

I have seen people healed almost immediately through prayer; however, in my experience prayer for healing must be ongoing. If I were Jesus, I could heal everyone in a minute, but I'm not Jesus. I'm more like a 1.5 volt battery trying to do the work of a huge dynamo (Jesus is the dynamo). At the same time, since the sacraments are the actions of Christ, there is a power at work in them that is greater than any power any human person has on their own. The power at work in the sacraments is the power of Christ.

Tonight after Mass I will offer the sacrament of the sick to anyone who wishes to receive it. It is for an illness that is more than just a simple cold, but a person need not wait until they are almost dead in order to ask for it. Like all the sacraments, it must be received with faith trusting that God is definitely present in the sacrament and in some way will touch the person receiving it with gracious love. Let us know also that we have some responsibility for our own health and we must take good care of ourselves and we should see a doctor when we need to. We cannot abuse our bodies by continuing to do things that are unhealthy and expect God to make everything right. As we continue the Mass, let us pray for the health and healing of all our parishioners and their families.

6th Sunday in Ordinary Time
February 12, 2006

INTRODUCTION – (Lev 13, 1-2. 44-46; 1 Cor. 13, 31 – 11, 1; Mark 1, 40-45) There are two chapters in the book of Leviticus on how to deal with leprosy. Many skin diseases in those days were lumped together under the diagnosis of leprosy. Quite possibly the person we hear about in today's gospel had ringworm, a type of a fungus. So many diseases of the skin were contagious that the person with such a disease had to be isolated from the community. It was not as humane as our isolation wards in the hospital. Actually they had to live outside the city and community, away from friends, family and their occupation. Usually they ended up living in caves or tombs. It was the priest's job to decide if a person was infected with this dreaded disease and if it seemed that a person's skin cleared up the priest had to pronounce that the person could re-enter society. Today in our first reading we hear a small section from the book of Leviticus that describes how to deal with a variety of skin diseases they referred to as leprosy. It prepares us for the gospel where Jesus was not afraid to touch a person infected with a skin disease, which would have made him unclean; but in touching the man he gave him back not only his health, but restored him to his home, his family and friends, his synagogue and his occupation.

HOMILY – I announced that today I would anoint the sick after Mass. I thought it was a good day to offer this sacrament because the gospel was about Jesus healing someone. However, in view of the weather, probably many of the people who would have come to be anointed decided to stay home. But there will be other opportunities after the weather turns a little warmer.

I administer the anointing of the sick to everyone I visit in the hospital or nursing home or to anyone I visit who is a shut-in. I make use of it frequently. I believe in the power of prayer and I believe in the power of this sacrament for the sick.

Recently I anointed a friend of mine who was going into the hospital. He was brought up in the old school when this sacrament was called Extreme Unction and he was a bit shocked when I suggested giving him the anointing. I don't think my explanation that this is a prayer and sacrament for the sick gave him much reassurance, because after I left him, he told his friends "I just received the last rites!" He might have thought he was a goner, but he wasn't. He's quite healthy today.

It was the Second Vatican Council that restored this sacrament to its original purpose: a prayer and sacrament for healing. Healing was part of Jesus' mission and also that of the disciples. When Jesus sent his disciples to help him in his work, St. Mark tells us they preached that people should turn away from their sins, they cast out demons and anointed many with oil and healed them. Even when physical healing is not the outcome, there is always some unique blessing and grace that comes with the sacrament.

Science had been pretty skeptical about faith and prayer until recently. Prayer is one of the liveliest areas of research in the field of alternative medicine today. For the past 15 or 20 years, science has started looking upon prayer more positively. Ten years ago Dr. Larry Dossey, a surgeon from Texas who didn't believe much in prayer for healing, started reviewing all the research on it and he ended up writing the book *Healing Words*. He concluded that prayer should be included with the prescriptions doctors write. An example of a more recent study was reported in October last year in Prevention Magazine. Dr. Mitchel Krucoff, a cardiologist at Duke University did a study with 150 men with heart problems. He concluded that, compared with a control group, those who were prayed for had a 50% reduction in heartbeat abnormalities and a 100% reduction in clinical outcomes such as heart attacks and heart failure. And none of the patients, their families, or the doctors treating them knew who was in the group being prayed for. I could bore you with other studies, but these studies appeal to the scientific side of my personality, because although I have faith in the power of prayer, I also had a good background in the scientific method when I studied experimental psychology.

So when I tell you prayer works, it's not just from what I believe, it's not just from what I have personally experienced (and I have had many personal experiences of the power of prayer), but I can support it from scientific research. It works. At the same time it is mysterious. We can't always control the outcome. And most of all, it doesn't happen as fast as we would like or as fast as it happens in the gospels. One thing

Jesus kept telling us over and over is to keep praying, to keep knocking. I think when we give up too soon, it shows we don't have very much faith in what prayer has the power to do for us. And we have to remember, when we pray, we are not dealing with inert substances, like using antibiotics to cure a bacterial infection. When we pray we are talking to our God whose wisdom and love is infinitely beyond our own. "Sometimes, God's operating from a larger script than yours," Dr. Frederick Flach says. Prayers are answered in many ways. On some occasions God may use illness for a purpose we do not understand. On other occasions, God may intervene directly and on still other occasions God may work through others, especially health care professionals. Although I've seen prayer bring immediate results, more times than not, it works better when we don't give up praying but keep at it. Keep knocking with faith. "Lord, if you want to, you can cure me."

7th Sunday in Ordinary Time
February 19, 2006

INTRODUCTION – (Isaiah 43, 18-19 21-22, 24b-25; 2 Cor. 1, 18-22; Mark 2, 1-12) When the Israelites left Egypt under Moses, they traveled through the Sinai desert and entered a land inhabited by the Canaanites. It was a wonderful experience to be free from Egyptian slavery and eventually to have a land and nation of their own. But often they allowed themselves to follow the pagan, sensuous customs of their Canaanite neighbors and this led to their undoing. Through their unfaithfulness to God their moral strength deteriorated and when the Babylonians attacked them in 597 B.C. they capitulated. They found themselves to be slaves and exiles once again and they knew they brought it on themselves. In today's first reading the prophet announces that God is about to set his people free again. He has forgiven their sins and their return will be so new and wonderful that they can forget about how he saved them from slavery the first time. Of course this was a slight exaggeration because their annual celebration of Passover constantly made them aware of God's saving them from slavery in Egypt and making them his people. Their liberation came when the Persians conquered the Babylonians and the king of Persia decreed in 538 B.C. that the Jews could return home.

Today's first reading is a good parallel to the gospel where Jesus forgave the sins of a paralytic then liberated him from his affliction. The second reading is a bit hard to understand, but it will make a little more sense if we realize Paul is defending himself against the charge of being wishy-washy.

HOMILY – I will begin with a true story. A man I knew was away from prayer, the Mass and the sacraments for a long time. He was also having problems with his marriage and with his work. Someone at work told him to read the Bible and it would help him. In desperation and as a last resort he picked up his bible and started reading. One idea began to emerge as he read through the Jewish history he found in the Old Testament. He noticed how many times the point was made that when the Jews forgot about God, things went badly for them. The Babylonian exile itself was the direct result of their having done exactly the opposite of what God told them to do. The man I'm telling you about concluded after reading the Bible that maybe things would go better for him if he got himself straightened out spiritually. So he did, and he told me both his marriage problems and his job situation improved beyond his expectations. More than that he was now at peace with himself.

In a similar way, Jesus in today's gospel put this man right with God before he gave him physical health. Not all sickness and suffering is indicative of a spiritual life that is ailing. But in the case of the paralytic, perhaps Jesus saw the one was somehow connected with the other.

Many people have the attitude that our health, our work, our family relationships have nothing to do with our relationship with God. They go to church on Sunday (if they do that much) then do as they please the rest of the week. Our faith teaches us all these areas of our lives are interconnected. In psychology there is a whole field of study called psychoneuro-immunology (I love that word – it makes me sound smart to say it!). This is also known as the mind-body connection. Our attitudes, beliefs, values, emotions can and do affect our health. And they affect how we deal with those we work with, live with and relate to. It might sound as if I've become a Christian Science minister if I say sin might cause sickness or suffering. I think sin is at the root of a lot of suffering in the world, suffering we bring on ourselves or suffering we cause others.

You know, in our journey through life, we all struggle with problems of one sort or another at times. It may be sickness. It may be the loss of a loved one. It may be inner turmoil. It may be caused by the cruelty or mistake of another. It doesn't matter whether a person is very holy or a terrible sinner, we're going to have difficulties. And I do not believe God uses sickness or suffering to punish us. Sometimes he might give us a push in the right direction, but life has enough problems of its own that God doesn't have to add to them. Our faith can bring us a lot of additional strength to deal with troubles. If we're not living the way God has taught us, we are going to add to our troubles. I say this simply because I believe God wants the best for us, and when we go in directions opposed to the way he has shown us, we are going against our own best self interest. Sin will affect us and it can paralyze us in many ways.

Although God condemns sin, God is merciful to the sinner and today's gospel gives us a message of hope. Christ came to save us from all those powers that want to pull us down, including sickness and death. If we find ourselves paralyzed in our relationship with God, Jesus is willing to help. He's always ready to extend mercy and help to those who come to him. And we don't have to tear the roof off of the church to get to him.

8th Sunday in Ordinary Time
February 26, 2006

INTRODUCTION – (Hosea 2, 16b. 17b. 21-22; II Cor. 3, 1b-6; Mark 2, 18-22) Our first reading today from the prophet Hosea goes back to a time of great material prosperity in Israel but also great spiritual collapse. God's people had forgotten their God and were ignoring the commandments. The image the prophet uses here is the image of marriage. In this image, God is represented as the faithful husband while Israel is his unfaithful spouse. Israel's unfaithfulness was in turning her affection and adoration to false gods. Although God's people were unfaithful, God would still be faithful. Even if he had to strip them of all their wealth and all their false gods and lead them into a desert, which he would do, he would do so in order to try to win them back to himself.

The reading leads into the gospel where Jesus uses the image of married love to answer a question about fasting. Implied in his answer is that he is the bridegroom, Israel's God.

HOMILY – God uses many different images to describe his love for us. One image God uses frequently is that of marriage. God wants to be close to us and wants us to be close to him in fidelity and joy.

In our gospel, some people, perhaps disciples of John the Baptist and the Pharisees, came to Jesus with a question about fasting. This question was not about the one day of fast that was required by law on the Day of Atonement. What is at issue here was a pious practice that the Pharisees and disciples of John the Baptist had of fasting in anticipation and preparation for the coming of the kingdom of God. Jesus' answer, in effect, was saying that there was no need for his disciples to fast since the kingdom had already come, in Jesus. Using the image of a wedding, Jesus compares himself to a bridegroom, a symbol that God used in the Old Testament for himself. Jesus implies that he is God among us who has come to reveal God's kingdom to us. He went on to tell the people who were questioning him that he would not always be among his people in a way that they could see him. "The days will come when the bridegroom is taken away from them, then they will fast..." In this statement the gospel is telling us that when we fast now, which we are invited to do beginning this Wednesday, it's not for the same reason that the Jews did it, in anticipation and preparation for God's coming to us. The bridegroom, our God, has come to us. We fast and sacrifice now in order to open ourselves more to his presence.

Our spiritual lives go in two directions; on the one hand we are called to celebrate because God is with us in Jesus (and the most perfect way we can celebrate this is in the Eucharist). On the other hand, however, we are required to discipline ourselves and make sacrifices because we know we have a lot of room to grow in order to be closer to our God. And so we have periods like Lent to help us grow and increase in God's love and grace.

There have been times in the past when I had just finished the consecration at Mass. As I looked at the host, I thought how simple this is: just say a few words and such a great miracle occurs; bread and wine become the body and blood of Christ. With just a few words Christ gives himself to all of us as our food and our drink. It seems almost too simple. [And for some it is too simple. They expect God to do things in a more dramatic, a more majestic way and they consequently miss the simple manner by which God chooses to act.] But as I thought of this simple miracle, I thought Christ must really want to be here with us, he must really want to give himself to us – that he made it all so simple.

In using the imagery of marriage in our readings today, God is speaking to us of his love. He is asking for our love. God has shown his love by taking on our flesh, by becoming human like us in every way except sin. He has shown us his love by dying for us, by not giving up on us, even when we give up on ourselves or give up on him. He has shown his love by sharing his Spirit with us and by giving himself to us in the Eucharist. He has shown his love by giving us hope that we will live forever with him in eternal joy if we follow the way he has shown us.

Let us praise his faithfulness and love and ask his help to respond with greater love.

1st Sunday of Lent
March 5, 2006

INTRODUCTION – (Gen. 9, 8-15; I Peter 3, 18-22; Mark 1, 12-15) We're going to hear the word "covenant" quite often in the next few Sundays. Today's first reading is about the covenant God made with Noah and his descendants which, according to the story, included all of us – the entire human race. A normal covenant would include promises two parties made to one another and expectations that the separate parties had of one another. The covenant God made with Noah is a one sided covenant in that God simply promises that he would never destroy the world by flood again, while he asks nothing of Noah in return. God gave the rainbow as a sign of his commitment to this covenant. St. Peter, in the second reading reminds us of a covenant God made with us at baptism. God would share his own life with us and our parents promised for us, or we ourselves promised if we were old enough, that we would be obedient and faithful sons and daughters of our Father, God. If we were too young to make those promises ourselves, as we grow older we have to make our own personal commitment to God if we hope to share in the blessings of God's covenant with us. One special sign God has given us to help us reaffirm our covenant with him is the Eucharist. [We have seven people from our parish who are making an important journey to enter into or to deepen their covenant with God through the Catholic Church. We are happy to have them with us. After the Prayer of the Faithful, we can send them off with our prayers to participate in the rite of election with the Archbishop this evening.]

HOMILY – Perhaps you heard the story about the priest who asked his parishioner, "do you find it difficult to resist temptation?" The parishioner answered, "I don't find it difficult at all, when it comes along, I just give in to it!"

The gospel for the first Sunday of Lent is always the gospel about Jesus spending 40 days in the desert being tempted and in fasting and prayer. St. Matthew and St. Luke give us a fuller description of Jesus' temptations. St. Mark gives us a very brief version, telling us only that Satan was there to tempt him. As we can see, whenever anyone, no matter who they are, is trying to love and serve God faithfully, Satan is there to see how he can keep it from happening.

This example of Jesus' fasting and praying is put before us as an inspiration for us as we begin Lent. It's hard to imagine that someone could totally fast for 40 days, but people have done it. St. Francis did. And St. Patrick would often go to a mountain in northern Ireland and spend the 40 days of Lent fasting and praying. The Church used to require all adult Catholics to observe a moderate kind of fast during Lent, but since Vatican II that obligation has been limited to Ash Wednesday and Good Friday. Many people think the Church is making it easier on us, but really the Church has made it more challenging. Fasting has a lot to recommend it, but it might be easier than doing other things we may need to do to grow in our love for God and our love for others. For example, it might be easier to give up dessert than to be kind to some obnoxious neighbor. Or it might be easier to give up candy and soft drinks than it would be to sit down and say a rosary every day. You might say to me: "But I really need to skip dessert or to give up candy and soft drinks." That may be true, but there's nothing that says we can't do more than one thing. The Church is asking us to take a serious look at ourselves and ask ourselves how we can be free from our addictions, our lack of charity, our negative attitudes or whatever.

Lent is a holy time, but it will only be holy for us if we make it holy. As Jesus tells us in today's gospel, "This is the time of fulfillment. The kingdom of God is at hand."

2nd Sunday of Lent
March 12, 2006

INTRODUCTION – (Genesis 22, 1-2. 9a. 10-13. 15-18; Romans 8, 31b-34; Mark 9, 2-10) Our stained glass window here in the sanctuary is an illustration of the story in our first reading of Abraham ready to sacrifice his son. Recall how God had made many promises to Abraham, promises that Abraham had to wait many years to see fulfilled. Among those promises was that he would be the father of a great nation. However, it wasn't until he and his wife Sarah were very old that his son Isaac was born. Several years after Isaac's birth, Abraham sensed God calling on him to offer up his son as a human sacrifice. Human sacrifice was not unusual at that time. Abraham loved Isaac. Just as an aside, this is the first time the word "love" appears in the bible. Besides his love for his son, Isaac was the fulfillment of all the hopes and promises God had made with Abraham. What could Abraham have thought? Did he displease God and God was canceling his promises? How could he kill his own son? But how could he disobey this God who had never let him down? I might point out a couple of interesting facts. Mt. Moriah is believed to be in Jerusalem, the very spot where King Solomon would build the Temple some 800 years later. As you know the Temple had a history of being destroyed and rebuilt a few times. The beautiful mosque called the Dome of the Rock now stands on that spot. It was built by followers of Mohammed in 690 A.D. It's the golden dome you often see when you look at a picture of Jerusalem. It is an issue over which the Jews and the Moslems are fighting today. The more conservative Jews want to tear it down and build a new temple in its place. The Moslems are determined not to let that happen.

HOMILY – Two mountains dominate our readings today: Mt. Moriah, the place where Abraham's faith was tested and another mountain, which was most likely Mt. Tabor, where Jesus was transfigured. I think these two mountains symbolize the ups and downs of every life. We have those times when our faith is tested, moments when we think God is demanding too much of us, moments when it seems God is asking us to give up all the blessings he had previously given us. And we have high moments, moments when God seems so close, when his presence fills us with wonder and awe, moments of blessing that we do not want to see come to an end. Often we have no control over where God might put us at different times in our lives: whether we find ourselves on Mt. Moriah facing great trials, or we find ourselves on Mt. Tabor in a state of ecstasy. But for most of us, most of the time we're somewhere in between, plugging along every day. Difficult times often seem to last forever but they seldom do. Abraham's time of trial ended when God said "hold off, you don't have to sacrifice your son. I just want to know you were willing to obey me." Sometimes that's all God wants from us is for us to say "Thy will be done." And the joyful moments in our lives end all too quickly. The apostles wanted to stay on Mt. Tabor forever but our Lord said it was time to go back down. There was a lot of work and very hard times ahead of him.

Not mentioned is a third very important mountain. It is foreshadowed in the story of Abraham and Isaac. God did not demand the human sacrifice of Isaac, but God's only son was to remain faithful to his mission even at the cost of his life on the hill of Calvary. Calvary also casts its shadow over the glory of Mt. Tabor. St. Mark makes an obvious connection between Jesus' passion and death and his transfiguration on Mt. Tabor. Mark tells us specifically the transfiguration took place six days after Jesus' first prediction of his passion and death. And Mark ends his narration of the transfiguration with Jesus telling Peter, James and John not to tell anyone of the vision until he had risen from the dead. The obvious linking of Jesus' death and resurrection with the transfiguration tells us that while Calvary reminds us of Jesus' suffering and his cross, it is also his hour of glory that brings us salvation, hope and peace.

The transfiguration was not only a revelation of the divinity hidden in Jesus but it was also a preview of his future glorification in the resurrection. It is also a preview of the glory God the Father wants us to share with his Son. The transfiguration is the fourth of the new mysteries of light for the rosary. As I was meditating on this mystery the other day I wondered how often the apostles experienced Jesus' glory like this? Only once and it was only three of them. They had to simply go on faith the rest of the time, seeing only the human side of Jesus who ate and slept and grew tired and was sometimes sad or angry just like them. Those special moments when we experience God's special closeness, when Jesus' presence is tangible to us, when our lives are touched by glory are few and far between. Most of the time we have to simply go on faith. But it is a faith that will lead to future glory. St. Paul asks us in today's second reading: "is it possible that he who did not spare his own Son but handed him over for the sake of us all will not grant us all things besides?"

3rd Sunday of Lent
March 19, 2006

INTRODUCTION – (Exodus 20, 1-17; I Cor. 1, 22-25; John 2, 13-25) Almost every Sunday during Lent this year, the first reading somehow relates to the theme of covenant. Two weeks ago we heard about God making a covenant with Noah and his descendants. In that covenant God promised he would never again destroy the world by water. Last week we heard about Abraham and the promises God made to him. Those promises were elements of God's covenant with Abraham. Today, the third Sunday of Lent, we hear about a third covenant, one that God made with his people as they were traveling through the desert on their way from Egypt to the Promised Land. In that covenant God promised his people liberty, land, prosperity and he promised them they would be his special people. Today's first reading tells us what God demanded of them in return. What God demanded of his people we call "The Ten Commandments." The first three or four are a little longer than what we're used to. We, who are Christians, still recognize these commands as obligations binding upon any nation that would hope to enjoy liberty, prosperity and God's special favor.

HOMILY – I would like to begin with a few details about today's gospel you might find interesting. From a historical point of view, the comment about the temple being under construction for 46 years is very helpful for figuring out about when it was that Jesus drove the merchants and moneychangers out of the Temple. Since other historical sources tell us when construction of the Temple began, we can figure that this event had to have happened sometime in 27 A.D. The gospels tell us it was at Passover time. Sacrifices of oxen, calves, sheep, goats and doves were sacrifices daily, but at Passover many thousands were sacrificed. From a strictly financial perspective, it was the major business activity in Jerusalem. In St. Mark's gospel we are told Jesus would not permit people to bring things through the Temple area. Apparently the merchants must have been transporting cattle, sheep and other items from place to place, using the Temple, where people were trying to pray, as a shortcut.

We do not know for sure at what point in Jesus' career this took place. St. John places it at the beginning of Jesus' public ministry while the other gospel writers place it at the end, right before Jesus' arrest and crucifixion. Most scholars believe St. John puts it at the beginning of Jesus' ministry because it highlights some of the themes St. John wanted to develop. It makes more sense to assume that it happened toward the end of Jesus' ministry and it's one of the things that led to his crucifixion and death.

I have already mentioned what a major industry this was. People who came from cities outside

Jerusalem would not have been able to bring animals with them to offer sacrifice, so they needed to purchase them when they arrived. The law required that people purchase their sacrifice with Jewish currency. Roman coins were considered idolatrous because they were engraved with pagan inscriptions and images. Since the Jews were under Roman occupation, they probably had to use Roman currency in their everyday lives. So when people came to Jerusalem and they wanted to buy an animal for sacrifice, they had to exchange their foreign money for Jewish currency. Thus we have the moneychangers who made their living by exchanging Roman currency for Jewish currency. One wonders how much profiteering was happening as the exchange was made.

No doubt there was a fair amount of price gouging in the sale of the animals for sacrifice. In the first three gospels, Jesus said they had turned God's house into a den of thieves. St. John didn't mention the den of thieves idea because he wanted to focus on reverence for God as was appropriate for such a holy place. This is the only time in the gospels we see Jesus act with such violence and anger.

Let us shift gears and talk about the commandments in today's first reading. Notice these weren't suggestions, they weren't options, they weren't modest proposals. The rules God made were very basic, but the way they are spoken is just as important as their content (what they should not do). Their format tells us they come from someone who is in charge. The first three commandments that stress worshipping God alone, respecting his name and keeping holy his name correspond with the gospel where Jesus was so angry about the irreverence shown to God in the Temple. What we see in both places is that we must keep God where he belongs in our lives, and where he belongs is on top.

Other than cleansing the Temple of all this business activity, honest and dishonest, there was something else Jesus did on this occasion. He made God accessible to everyone. He broke down the wall that divided Jews and Gentiles. Gentiles had been forbidden under pain of death to enter the temple and so were the blind and the lame. On this occasion Jesus quoted Isaiah "my house will be called a house of prayer for all peoples." And that access would be through Jesus. He said as much when he said: "Destroy this temple and in three days I will raise it up." This work of making access to God available to all people would take place especially through the death and resurrection of Jesus, an event we share in each time we come to Mass.

The commandments and the cleansing of the Temple come to us today on this third Sunday of Lent to ask us to reflect on our own relationship with God. We call him Lord. Do our lives show that we believe what we say?

4th Sunday of Lent
March 26, 2006

INTRODUCTION – (2 Chronicles 36, 14-16.19-23; Eph. 2, 4-10; John 3, 14-21) Our first reading last Sunday was about the covenant God made with his people as they were traveling through the desert on their way from Egypt to the Promised Land. In that covenant God promised his people liberty, land, prosperity and he promised them they would be his special people. What God demanded of his people in return was obedience to his commandments, especially the ones we call "The Ten Commandments." Our first reading this week skips over seven centuries, centuries marked with religious fervor at times, but mostly characterized by indifference to God and to his laws. This indifference took its toll on their strength as a nation and when the powerful Babylonians came against God's people around 600 B.C. they were unable to defend themselves. As a result their land was destroyed and those who managed to survive the Babylonian invasion were enslaved and deported to Babylon. Today's first reading describes this calamity and how God freed them from their Babylonian captivity almost two generations later. Their liberation from Babylon took place when the Persian king, Cyrus, conquered the Babylonians. Just to help you visualize this, Persia was the land now occupied by Iran and Babylonia was in modern day Iraq. One last thought: next week we will hear Jeremiah promise that God would make a new covenant with his people since the old one was so poorly kept. We celebrate and renew God's new covenant as always as we celebrate the Eucharist today.

HOMILY – One of the central elements of our relationship with God is the idea of covenant. The word "covenant" is not a word we use everyday. It is a solemn and serious agreement, but it is more that that. It is a committed relationship between two people or two groups of people. About the only time we hear the word "covenant" today is in relation to marriage. But in the Bible we hear the word a lot. Last Sunday, this Sunday and next Sunday, in our first reading, we hear passages that referred to the covenant God made with his people. The author of the first reading tells us this covenant was broken more often than it was observed. Instead of giving up on us, however, God offered us a new covenant, sealed in the blood of his Son. It's a covenant we renew and God renews with us every time we come to Mass.

God offers this new covenant to all people. As Jesus said: "God gave his only Son so that everyone who believes in him might not perish, but might have eternal life." But not all people want to enter into a covenant of love with this God who sent his son. Again he tells us: "The light came into the world, but people preferred the darkness to light..."

God is our creator who knows us better than we know ourselves. He knows what is for our good, he knows what will lead us to peace and life, eternal life, but he also gave us a free will. He gave us a free will so we would be capable of returning his love. Only a free person can love. But with our free will we can also choose not to love. And making that choice not to love our God points us in a direction that leads away from eternal life and eternal happiness.

People with a concept of "covenant" (even if they've never heard the word "covenant," but who know they are in a relationship of love with God) know a God whom we can call Father, lover, spouse, friend, protector or savior. Without a notion of "covenant" we cannot really know God in a personal way. Without a notion of "covenant" God is seen perhaps as indifferent, overly punitive or overly permissive. I think most people today, who have no notion of "covenant," see God as some kind of indulgent parent who doesn't know how to say "no" and who is so soft hearted he's going to get everyone into heaven no matter how evil they may have been. Jesus did say "God did not send his son into the world to condemn the world," but he also said that whoever does not believe in him is already condemned because they preferred darkness to light. Jesus has done all that is possible, even to the extent of dying for us, so that we can discover the light, the life, the joy that his love can bring, but he cannot force it on us if we are closed to it.

I want to say something about baptism because that's when we begin to live a new life, when we receive the light of Christ, when we enter into a covenant relationship with God. Often I have asked people when they come for the baptism of their child why they want their child baptized. The most common answer is because it washes away original sin. Those who have a deeper understanding of baptism tell me it is because baptism gives their child a sharing in Christ's life. But even that answer is incomplete. Let me draw a comparison between baptism and natural birth. When a child is born, we say they are given the gift of life (although they had already received that gift at conception). But we also know that there's a lot more to being born than simply receiving the gift of life. Natural birth is the beginning of a lengthy, complex process of growth, development, learning and maturation. So too is baptism the beginning of a process of growing in God's love, learning to recognize God as our Father, learning to obey him, worship him, love him, pray to him. That describes a loving relationship with our God that is meant to continue into eternity. One word for that relationship is "covenant." When we come to Mass each week, we come so we don't forget our covenant, that we are sharers in God's life; so we don't forget what Christ has done for us and what he asks of us in this relationship of love. We all know and God knows too how easily we forget things, so he gave us a way to remember: "Do this in memory of me." Thank you for being here today to hear once more of God's love and to express your own love in prayer and praise. Amen.

5th Sunday of Lent
April 2, 2006

(Ezekiel 37, 12-14; Romans 8, 8-11; John 11, 1-45) Jesus had recently raised his dead friend, Lazarus, back to life. The raising of Lazarus took place in Bethany, a village just a couple of miles outside of Jerusalem. Today's gospel takes place on Palm Sunday in Jerusalem. When they heard Jesus was coming to Jerusalem, many who were impressed with Jesus' miracles, especially the raising of Lazarus, and many who were there to celebrate Passover, gathered around him and escorted him into Jerusalem with palms, chanting "Hosanna to the Son of David." When Jesus' enemies saw this, they were filled with jealousy and said to one another: "We've lost! Look! The whole world has gone after him." This is where the events in today's gospel begins. The gospel tells us some Greeks who had come to worship at the Passover feast wanted to see Jesus. Jerusalem would swell with worshippers during the great feasts - especially the feast of Passover. People from distant places would often come several days ahead of time so they could find a place to stay. This request from foreigners, non-Jews, to see Jesus was a sign to him his hour had come. He had come to save all people and he knew that he had to die in order to reach all people. He knew his death would be the most tortuous form of death ever devised by human beings, yet he refers to it as his glorification. "The hour has come for the Son of Man to be glorified." He would be glorified in his faithfulness to his Father's work, he would be glorified in laying down his life for all of us whom he loves (greater love than this, no one has than that he lay down his life for his friends.) He would be glorified in his resurrection.

In calling it his glorification, Jesus was being brave with six days yet to go before his death, but we hear also his struggle in today's gospel. "I am troubled now," he said. "Yet what should I say? 'Father, save me from this hour'? But it was for this purpose that I came to this hour." That sounds very much like Jesus' prayer in the Garden of Gethsemani the night before he died. We hear of Jesus' struggle in today's second reading too: "he offered prayers and supplications with loud cries and tears to the one who was able to save him from death…"

When I was in Israel, visiting the Garden of Gethsemani, I could see how easy it would have been for Jesus to walk away that night. Jesus could have taken the steps going up the side of the Mount of Olives to Bethany and been with his friends, Martha, Mary and Lazarus, in less than an hour. He could have gotten some food and water and disappeared into the wilderness for a few days. The Roman soldiers would not have wasted their time to go after him. They had no quarrel with him. He could have quietly returned to Galilee to lead a simple life working in a carpentry shop somewhere and no one would have heard of him again. His apostles would have dispersed and all his healings and his teachings about God's love and salvation would have been quickly forgotten. But his mission was to save the world, not himself. He would have betrayed his Father, his mission and himself had he run away.

Like a seed planted in the ground, he had to die to what he was in order to live in a new way. He had to die to this life so he could fill the whole world with his presence and his grace.

This is the new covenant Jeremiah tells us about in today's first reading, a covenant written in our hearts.

The covenant becomes a part of us because he becomes a part of us through his Holy Spirit and we become a part of him. That union is deepened each time we pray, each time we love unselfishly, each time we are faithful to our mission in life, each time we celebrate the Eucharist and participate in the blood of the new and eternal covenant.

Jesus had the option of taking what appeared to be the easy way out. Even then, his decision to stand by what he did and taught was hard. He warns us that sometimes it's hard for us, too, to do what we have to do. We just heard him say in the gospel: "Whoever loves his life loses it, and whoever hates his life in this world will preserve it for eternal life." This was literally true for many of Christ's followers. Many people had to give up their lives to remain faithful to Christ. Gratefully in this land today, we do not have to sacrifice our life for our faith, but to be faithful is not always the easiest path. Coming to Mass on Sunday, staying chaste, being honest, doing for others, forgiving injuries, loving our neighbor, especially the obnoxious ones, is not always easy.

Today's gospel is essentially a theological reflection on the cross, Jesus' cross and ours. Let us ask our Lord to help us remain faithful and know that all crosses are temporary, while the glory of union with Christ and following his lead is eternal.

Passion Sunday
April 9, 2006

(Isaiah 50, 4-7; Phil 2: 6-11; Mark 14, 1 – 15, 47) We hear today from St. Mark, the earliest and the shortest of our gospels. There are only 16 chapters in the whole gospel. Yet almost one third of his gospel (five chapters) describes what happened in the last week of Jesus' life, from his triumphal entry into Jerusalem on Palm Sunday until his resurrection on Easter Sunday. St. John has even more of his gospel devoted to the passion-resurrection narrative. St. John's gospel devotes almost the entire second half of his gospel to this one week in Jesus' life here on earth.

Here is the reason for pointing this out. Everything Jesus did and said during three years of public ministry was important, but the events of his life from Palm Sunday to Easter Sunday, events we commemorate this coming week are the most important of all. For some people Christmas may seem to be the most important feast in the entire year, with all the celebrations that happen around that time. Certainly the birth of Jesus is worth celebrating with great joy, but we would not have even heard of Jesus if it hadn't been for the events that happened between Palm Sunday and Easter Sunday. If you miss out on what we commemorate this week, you are missing out on the main event on which our faith is built. I invite you to come to whatever services you can come to. If you can't come to services, please try to put some time aside and get out your bibles and read and pray about what happened to Jesus between Palm Sunday and Easter Sunday. Easter Sunday will not have much depth of meaning for us without an awareness of what Jesus said and did this week.

We hear a lot today about a few gospels that carry such biblical names as: the gospels of Thomas, of the Hebrews, of the Egyptians, of Mary, of Peter, of Philip and now the latest, the gospel of Judas. They give us interesting and sometimes even bizarre interpretations of the life of Jesus. We have to remember the word gospel means "good news" and it is the good news of salvation Jesus taught through his life, death and resurrection. And what Jesus did and taught was preached by apostles who were witnesses of Jesus' life (and by the way, the Greek word for witness is 'martyr'). The gospel was preached and taught for twenty or thirty years before anything was written down. These strange gospels we've been hearing about were written much later than the original four we have and they were largely ignored by the early Church, not as a power struggle or to hide any arcane truths, but because they did not reflect the original teachings of the apostles and they did not reflect the faith of the early Christian Community.

The four gospels the Church has preserved and taught have given Christians through the centuries a vision of Jesus that was considered authentic and true from earliest times. They have given Christians something secure to hold on to in the ups and downs of life. Through the gospels we know that God's love can and will overcome all evil and even death itself. That's the good news. Our Lord often doesn't run the world the way we think he should. He doesn't always give us everything we want. But in trying times he will always be with us, if we open our hearts to him. I know what a strength meditation on the suffering, death and resurrection of Jesus has always been for me.

I recommend you take your palm home today. Keep it somewhere where you'll see it from time to time to remind you Jesus entered Jerusalem knowing fully what was ahead for him. Let it remind you of Jesus' courage, his faithfulness to his mission, his victory over sin and death. Let it remind you of his love for you and for me.

Holy Thursday
April 13, 2006

I have come across statistics, and I'm sure many of you have too, about memory: how the percent of what we remember from what we read and what we hear is rather small, while we remember a very high percent of the things we do. God, of course, knew that long before statisticians showed up on the face of the earth, and so in order that we would remember the things he wanted us to remember, he gave us things to do.

Our first reading this evening (Exodus 12, 1-8.11-14) took us back 1300 years before Christ, when the Hebrew people were on the run, fleeing slavery in Egypt, on their way to a new life of freedom in a promised land. While on their journey God revealed himself to them. He told them of the special love he would have for them and how they were to love him and love one another. And God did not want them to forget this, so he gave them something to do so that they would always remember. Their annual Passover celebration would help them remember what God had done for them and what God wanted them to do in turn. We heard in today's first reading God telling his people: "This day shall be a memorial feast for you which all your generations shall celebrate with pilgrimage to the Lord as a perpetual institution."

We are not slaves of a foreign country like the Jews were 1300 years before Christ, but many of us still find ourselves on the run, having places to go, things to do, people to see and meetings to attend. God does not want us either to forget what he has done for us and what he wants us to do in turn. When we're on the run all the time it's very easy to forget these things. So God gave us things to do to help us remember.

Just as the Jews celebrated God's love for them at a special meal, so it is at a special meal that we are to remember and celebrate God's love for us. That meal is called the Eucharist (a word which means appropriately enough: "thanksgiving"). In tonight's second reading (I Cor. 11, 23-26) St. Paul gives us the earliest written account of the Eucharist. We are to come together to eat and drink the body and blood of our Lord. And in this short passage we are told twice: "Do this in remembrance of me."

In tonight's gospel we hear about another thing we are to do: "As I have done, so you must do..." (Jn. 13, 1-15). At the time of Jesus, people wore sandals and they didn't have cars. Lots of animals traveled on the same roads people walked on, so you can imagine their feet got pretty dusty and dirty. If you came to someone's house for dinner or they came to your house, it wouldn't be pleasant for the guest to have to sit though a nice meal with smelly dirty feet. So it was standard procedure when a guest came, someone washed the guest's feet, usually a servant, or if there were no servants, one of the children had that nasty job. The fact that the need no longer exists in this day and age does not mean we are off the hook when Jesus tells us "as I have done, so you must do..." There are lots of other gracious and hospitable and humbling things we can do for one another instead of washing feet. And so our foot washing tonight is a mere symbol to help us remember how we are to serve one another.

These two things we are to do, the celebration of the Eucharist and washing of the feet, not only help us remember what God has done for us but also what God expects of us in turn. And in these two things we have an expression of two virtues essential to our relationship with God: faith and love. Let me say a word about each one. First faith: I am sure your faith is tested every time you hear those words: "This is my body." "This is my blood." My faith is tested too. Every morning I am called to believe those words, believing that God has given to human beings, to people like me, the power to change bread and wine into the flesh and blood of Jesus Christ. It was a test failed by many people who initially followed Jesus. When Jesus first spoke to his followers about the Eucharist, St. John tells us many left him at that point. When they walked away he didn't call them back to say they misunderstood him. He knew they were leaving him precisely because they did understand him. All he did was ask the apostles if they were going to leave too. We all know how Peter responded: "Lord, to whom would we go? You alone have the words of eternal life."

The second virtue essential in our relationship with God is love. Jesus had been doing a servant's work all his life, healing and teaching, even to the point that sometimes he and his apostles couldn't find time to rest or even to eat. In serving others, washing feet was probably a piece of cake for him. The hardest job he would have would happen on the next day when he would give his life for us. Is it possible we would ever have to go that far for one another? Sometimes. What mother or father wouldn't put their life at risk for their child. And whenever I have the funeral of a veteran, I am always deeply moved when I see that American flag draping the casket. I am touched to realize that this person was willing to risk his or her life for me, for my safety and security and freedom. But even if we're not called to give up our life for someone else, when we recall Jesus' love it prompts us to respond by loving him more and by trying to be more loving toward one another.

Many of us feel that we're running all the time.

And so to help us remember there's more to life than stress and pressure, Jesus gave us two things to do to help us remember. We are to share a special meal that will sustain us spiritually, just as the food we eat each day sustains us physically and we are to serve one another in humility and love. Tonight we remember when it all began.

Easter
April 16, 2006

When England was fighting Napoleon at the battle of Waterloo, the English government had signs placed in a variety of cities to let the citizens of Great Britain know how the war was going. One such sign was on the bell tower of Winchester Cathedral. When the sign went up that summer day in 1815, it was partly obscured by cloud and fog, but the people could see enough of the sign to be able to read: "England defeated." Everyone who saw it felt defeated too, until the cloud lifted and they could see the whole sign which read: "England defeated Napoleon." Within seconds, their sorrow was turned into joy and defeat was swallowed up in victory.

When Jesus died on the cross, those who believed in him felt lost and defeated. Jesus was dead and so were their hopes for a better world. But in just a couple of days their sorrow was turned into joy and defeat was swallowed up in victory.

A fourth grade teacher planned to perform an Easter pageant for the parents of her students. Every boy and girl had a part to play. After all the parts were given out, the last child to receive a part was Johnny. He got to be the stone in front of the tomb. No special costume was required for this part. All he had to do was to roll him self into a ball and pretend to be the stone. The teacher felt sorry for Johnny since all the other children got to wear costumes so before the final performance she asked Johnny if he wanted another part so he could wear a costume. Johnny did not want to change. He said: "it's the most important part. If the stone doesn't roll away, then nobody can get into the tomb and see that it is empty."

A very smart little boy! The stone had to be moved away not so Jesus could get out. He had already risen and was out of there. The stone had to be removed for us so that we could see the tomb was empty; so we could see that death had been robbed of its power; so we could see that a new world order had begun; so we could see the truth in Jesus' words: "I am the resurrection and the life."

At Easter we see lilies, Easter baskets, colored eggs, Easter bunnies, new outfits, etc., but the main symbol is the empty tomb, now in the Church of the Holy Sepulcher in Jerusalem. We've all seen artistic interpretations of the resurrection, but no one but the Roman guards were there when it happened and they reported it only to the high priests. The only evidence we have of the resurrection is an empty tomb and many eyewitness accounts of people who saw him after his resurrection, people who were willing to go to their death to witness that he was alive and they indeed did see him.

Those who saw him knew that what they were seeing was entirely different than anything they had ever seen before. Jesus was not just a dead man who had come back again to live the life he had before. He came back to a new kind of life, one that is beyond our ability to relate to so it is shrouded in mystery for us, and yet it is very real. He could be seen and touched, he could eat food with his friends, he could move from one place to another effortlessly, walls and locked doors could not keep him in or out and those who saw him reported he even looked different. Yet when they saw him they knew it was no one else but the Lord.

His friends eventually came to know that when they saw him, his resurrection was more than God's endorsement on his good life. They knew his resurrection had something to do with them. The young man at the tomb told the women "he is going before you to Galilee." (Mk. 16, 1-7) His friends came to know that he was always ahead of us and was always going before us, calling us to follow him. He is our good shepherd, guiding us to new life. His resurrection was not just a personal favor to Jesus. It is a preview for each and every one of us who will allow ourselves to be guided by his word and sacraments.

When Jesus told his friend Martha when her brother died: "I am the resurrection and the life," he added: "whoever believes in me, even if he dies, will live, and whoever lives and believes in me will never die." Because of this St. Paul tells us today: "If then you were raised with Christ, seek what is above, where Christ is seated at the right hand of God. Think of what is above, not of what is on earth." (Coloss. 3, 1-4)

Jesus overcame the power of evil and death in his resurrection. This does not mean evil and death no longer exist in the world. And because they do exist, many people discount Jesus' resurrection. It is true, the resurrection has not removed evil and death from the face of the earth, but it tells us evil and death will not have the last word. They are not the final outcome; they cannot ultimately defeat us if we share Christ's life. Today we celebrate Jesus' victory and our own. "This is the day the Lord has made. Let us rejoice and be glad." Amen.

2nd Sunday of Easter
April 23, 2006

(Acts 4, 32-35; 1 John 5, 1-6; John 20, 19-31) The chief rabbi in Jerusalem contacted the Holy Father and invited him to a game of golf. He thought it would be a good gesture for improved Jewish-Christian relations. The Holy Father agreed with the idea but said he wasn't a good golfer, so he asked if he if he could send a high level prelate to be his substitute. That was agreeable with the chief rabbi. He consequently asked around among his cardinals whether any of them were good golfers so they could stand in as his representative. None of them felt they could do the job, but one of the cardinals suggested Jack Nicklas. He told the Holy Father that Jack Nicklas was a good Catholic and perhaps the Holy Father could make him a cardinal. So that's what the Holy Father did. He made Jack Nicklas a cardinal and he was the Holy Father's representative for this big inter-religious golf game. When it was over Cardinal Jack Nicklas called the Holy Father and the Holy Father asked how it went. Jack answered "I've got good news and bad news for you." The Holy Father said "Well, start with the good news." So Jack told him: "it was the best game I ever played. I felt like God was right there with me on every stroke. It couldn't have been better." "Well," asked the Holy Father, how could there be bad news after that?" Jack Nicklas answered "I lost by two strokes to Rabbi Tiger Woods."

In some corners of the world this is known as holy humor Sunday. It's a day for laughter, because the devil got defeated by Jesus' resurrection. So I had to tell you something that would give you a laugh.

Some of you might also know this Sunday as "Divine Mercy Sunday," when Jesus forgave his apostles for abandoning him and offered them "peace." He also commissioned them to bring his mercy and salvation to others by giving them the power to forgive sins.

The gospel talks to us too about Jesus giving the apostles the gift of the Holy Spirit and the apostle Thomas and his doubts and, more importantly, his profound expression of faith. There are so many ideas my homily could develop.

What I want to focus on is Jesus' greeting to the apostles: "peace be with you." When we read the gospels, the normal greeting was "Χαίρε" which means "rejoice!" Jesus obviously meant "peace" because he repeated it.

This gospel has a great deal of meaning for me personally and I'm going to tell you why. I was ordained almost 42 years ago, just as the Vatican Council was finishing up its work. People had high hopes for all the changes that the Vatican Council might bring. Perhaps they envisioned a Church such as we read about in today's first reading, where there was great unity and peace and love for each other. Vatican II did great work, but about five or ten years after the Council was over, it was obvious it didn't do everything people expected. Most people were happy with the changes it brought about. But there were some who liked the old ways and they were disgruntled. Some stopped going to Church and some broke away from the Church and began their own Church. Others were upset because there weren't more changes and they turned away from the Church also.

It was a difficult time for me as a priest too. Priests I knew and admired resigned. Some of the pastors I had to serve under didn't like the changes from the Vatican Council and they saw me as a wild liberal they had to try to keep in line. I was thirty years old by then and I was told when to come in at night, how to dress, who to have as friends, and for my weekly "day off" I was permitted to visit my parents on Friday night after I had finished my day's chores. By 30 years of age I thought I knew everything and resented someone telling me how to live my life. Our seminary professors assured us that if we studied our theology we could handle any situation. I guess it was troubling to find out that I still had a lot to learn.

I'm not looking for sympathy. I'm just trying to give you a picture of my own internal distress. I had no inner peace. At that time I felt restless, depressed and disturbed. At charismatic prayer meetings I heard people give testimony of how God answered their prayers. Yet I was so troubled and when I prayed I felt as if God wasn't listening. Perhaps I wasn't listening well enough. But one day I listened as someone read today's gospel. It was one of those moments when I knew God was speaking to me. I heard it loud and clear: "Peace be with you." It didn't come all at once, but hearing those words of the risen Jesus gave me hope. It assured me "peace" was something God wanted for us, and I prayed for it with greater conviction that it would come. I knew it would come because Jesus desires us to have it. Just knowing that was the beginning of a feeling of peace. As I prayed for it, the Lord guided me as to how to find it. I tell you this story so that you might know that God wants peace for us. It was what he promised at the Last Supper: "Peace I leave with you; my peace I give to you. Not as the world gives do I give it to you. Do not let your hearts be troubled or afraid."

That is my prayer for all of you this second Sunday of Easter: may you know and experience Christ's peace, a peace which the world cannot give. Amen.

3rd Sunday of Easter
April 30, 2006

(Acts 3, 13-15. 17-19; 1 John 2, 1-5a; Luke 24, 35-48) A mother proudly told her pastor: "My teenage son has finally learned one bible verse. It's Luke 24, verse 41 where Jesus asks his disciples (as we just heard in today's reading) 'Do you have anything here to eat?'"

The apostles must have been in great confusion by Easter Sunday night. Jesus' tomb was empty. Peter and John had seen the empty tomb in the morning, but they had seen nothing else. Some women, who were Jesus' followers, had talked with an angel who assured them Jesus had risen. Mary Magdalene herself had seen our Lord. Later in the day Jesus appeared to two other disciples, walked and talked with them, broke bread with them and then disappeared. Those same disciples had just arrived at where the apostles were staying and were telling their story when Jesus suddenly appeared to all of them. Surprised, shocked, disbelief, St. Luke says "terrified," probably embarrassed, too, realizing they had all abandoned him after his arrest. What a mixed bag of emotions they must have been experiencing. No wonder he greets them by saying to them: "Peace be with you." Jesus dispels their doubts about whether they could believe what they were seeing and assures them they are not seeing a ghost by inviting them to feel him, to know that he is flesh and bone. He even ate a piece of fish, food they themselves had prepared, to prove to them that he was real and that he had really risen. And yet he appeared to be different than before. The wounds of the nails and the spear were still in his hands and feet and side. But when he appeared to Mary Magdalene she didn't recognize him until he spoke her name. The two disciples didn't recognize him until he sat down and broke bread with them. There was no doubt it was Jesus, but he was different.

He not only looked different, but he was different in other ways too. He didn't come knocking on their door in order to get in. He just suddenly stood in their midst. The same thing happened with the others who saw him. When his visit to Mary or the two disciples or the apostles had come to an end, he simply vanished. It was as if he was always with them, and sometimes he allowed them to see him but most of the time they couldn't.

Human beings have invented all kinds of marvelous things. There are great discoveries in medicine that can add years to people's lives. There are wonderful inventions that can make life much more comfortable and enjoyable. We can walk on the moon and we can explore the atom. We have powerful weapons that can cause untold destruction. But who has ever discovered how to overcome the power of death which every living thing must eventually succumb to? The resurrection of Jesus is the most fantastic event that this world could ever know. Since the days when human beings lived in caves, all our inventions, all our discoveries, all our power added together cannot begin to equal the glory of Christ's resurrection that introduced into our world and our history new and eternal life.

The resurrection celebrated not just Jesus' glory but our own future glory if we will open our minds and hearts to him. Jesus' resurrection is a preview of God's plans for those who are his children in Christ. Is this one of those "something for nothing" offers? Have you ever received a phone call where someone said to you: "Mrs. Jones, I have good news for you, or I have this free gift for you!" I usually say, thank you, I'm not interested! We always know when someone we don't know wants to give us something for free, he wants something. Is religion giving us something for free? The answer is "yes" and "no." The answer is "yes" in the sense that God's life offered to us in Jesus is not something we have earned or merited. It is a free gift. That's why it's called "grace," the Latin word for gift. At the same time God does want something from us. Eternal life is not automatic. We are not saved without our participation and our cooperation. What does God want? It's simple. He wants us to give up our sins. He tells us this in all three of today's readings. In the first reading, St. Peter tells us: "repent, therefore, and be converted." St. John tells us in the second reading we have to keep God's commandments. Jesus, when he was talking with the apostles, told them to preach "repentance for the forgiveness of sins." God is not really asking too much of a sacrifice from us because it's our sins that keep us from the peace and happiness and joy God wants us to have. Remember it was sin that created problems for the human race in the beginning. God created Adam and Eve to be happy as was symbolized by the Garden of Eden. It was because of their sin that they lost that happiness.

A special help God gives us to keep us close to him, in his grace and in his peace, is the Eucharist. The fact that Christ gives himself to us as food tells us something. It tells us we always need him. A person can't eat just every now and then. We have to constantly feed this body of ours if we are going to stay healthy and have the energy we need to get through each day. Jesus is telling us we can't just come to him every now and then. We need his help all the time. So today we come to him again to be taught, to be fed, to be touched by his loving presence. We ask him to keep us filled with the life he has given us and which we hope to share in for all eternity.

4th Sunday of Easter
May 7, 2006

INTRODUCTION – In the Acts of the Apostles, we are told about Peter and John healing a crippled beggar in the Temple. Once the man was healed, he was so excited that he could walk he started jumping and running around. You can imagine this caused quite a stir in the Temple. People wanted to know how he was cured and the apostles started telling them about Jesus. Very quickly the apostles were arrested for preaching about Jesus. The leaders wanted everyone to forget about Jesus and so they dragged the apostles into court. Today's first reading is Peter's statement before the Jewish leaders. (Acts 4, 8-12)

HOMILY – "There is no salvation in anyone else, for there is no other name in the whole world given to people by which we are to be saved." These words conclude today's first reading. It was part of St. Peter's speech to the Jewish leaders who had put him on trial for healing a crippled man in the name of Jesus.

"There is no salvation in anyone else..." Several years ago I had a discussion with a lady in another parish. She had a daughter in our parish school, a little girl for whom our parish was paying most of the tuition. I never saw the mother or daughter in church on Sunday so I decided to have a little talk with her about it. She said her daughter was significantly involved in gymnastics and then she told me, "Gymnastics is her salvation!" I was too stunned to know what to say to this person who claimed to be a good Catholic. She missed something along the way of her spiritual journey. St. Peter would not have had any difficulty responding to that statement. He would have said "there is no salvation in anyone else..." other than Jesus.

Now I'm not going to bash sports or athletics. I'm not much of a spectator, but I used to play lots of sports before I hurt my knee: softball, handball, racquetball, tennis, ice skating, roller skating, swimming, bowling (when I was in the seminary I had charge of taking care of the bowling alleys). I even tried to play polo. I stayed on the horse pretty well, but I was lousy trying to hit that polo ball. Participation in sports has a lot of benefits, and for a select few they can mean big bucks. But they are no one's salvation in the fullest sense of the word.

Almost everyone remembers the first commandment: "I am the Lord thy God, thou shalt not have strange gods before me." I doubt that anyone has a golden statue of Jupiter or Mars sitting around their house to which they burn incense. But there are other kinds of idols. Idols can take the form of sports or the TV, or money, or pride, or lust, or laziness, or addictions or any form at all. Even doing God's work can pull us away from God. There are times when I let myself become so busy that my necessary prayers get neglected. Anything can become an idol when it becomes more important than God himself, when it pushes God into a secondary or inferior place in our lives. There are many areas of our lives that are important, but God has to be there too. As we get closer to God, God may invite us to become more and more generous with ourselves in our love for him and for others, but there are some basic bottom line rules which he expects us to follow and which are not at all unreasonable or excessively demanding.

Today Jesus tells us he is the good shepherd. (Jn. 10, 11-18) He is a shepherd who is dedicated to his sheep. He cares about his sheep and not about getting a paycheck. He tells us he knows each of us individually and is willing to risk his life for us. He did lay down his life for us. Shepherds are not so common today, so the image does not grab us like it would have touched Jesus' listeners 2000 years ago. But there is another image Jesus used a lot, an image that is similar to the shepherd image and an image we can all relate to - the image of a loving parent.

As a Father and a shepherd he guides us. One of the ways he guides us is through his word that teaches us and the sacrament of the Eucharist that nourishes us. His love is greater than we can imagine and in his love he wants us to follow his lead for "there is no salvation in anyone else..."

5th Sunday of Easter
May 14, 2006

INTRODUCTION – (Acts 9, 26-31; I John 3, 18-24; John 15, 1-8) Many of the Jews, because they were under Roman occupation, had two names - a Jewish name and a Roman name. Thus St. Paul also had the name Saul. Most of the time he is called Paul, but occasionally, as in today's first reading, he is called Saul. You remember he was a zealous Pharisee and a fierce persecutor of all who believed in Christ. As a matter of fact, it was when he was traveling to Damascus to arrest Christians there, that Jesus appeared to him and convinced him he was all wrong. His life turned around completely and he started preaching and teaching about Jesus. Even after three years in Damascus, preaching that Jesus was the Son of God, the Christian community in Jerusalem was not convinced that he was for real. When he first showed up in Jerusalem, as we hear in today's first reading, they still didn't trust him.

HOMILY – A mother and father who had been married to one another for 45 years were living in California. They had a son who lived in New York and a daughter who lived in Chicago. It was the day before Mothers' Day and the father called his son and told him: "I have bad news for you. After 45 years of misery, your mother and I are calling it quits. We're getting a divorce." The son went ballistic. He tried to tell his father they couldn't do that. He called his sister and they both decided to fly to California right away to talk to their parents and straighten them out. They called their folks and told them they would be there the next day. The father hung up the phone, turned to his wife and said "the kids will be home for Mothers' Day and they are paying their own way!"

Happy Mothers' Day to all our mothers. I hope you get a visit from your children or at least a phone call. There was a short article in US News and World Report recently that said if stay-at-home moms were to be compensated according to what they are worth, they would command a salary of over $134,000 a year. As for working moms, they deserve to be paid nearly $86,000 a year just for their household duties, including those of chef, accountant, teacher, chauffer, and nurse. Of course a mother's true worth can't be measured in dollars and cents; they are priceless.

Today on Mothers' Day we recall one of the people who gave us life. Some times when people get older they want to know even more about their origins. At least once or twice a week we get phone calls asking us if we have records about someone's grandparents, great grand parents or even further back. I only wish I had asked and had written down more about my own ancestors before my parents had died.

Jesus is telling us today about our spiritual ancestry in the image of the vine and the branches. In a typical family tree, one generation brings new life into the world and then they pass on. Those who gave us life leave us to survive on our own and on what they taught us.

Jesus' example shows us that even though he is the source of our spiritual life, we are always dependent on him just as a branch depends on the vine. Christ never leaves us to survive on our own. If we were to become separated from him spiritually we would be dead. Without me you can do nothing he tells us.

Did you ever notice how many ways Jesus tried to tell us we need to stay close to him? Last Sunday we heard him tell us "I am the good shepherd." Sheep need their shepherd to survive. He told us "I am the bread of life." We need food to live. He told us "I am the light of the world." Picture trying to get around without light. If suddenly a dense cloud would cover the earth, not only would it be difficult to move around but life as we now know it would eventually disappear.

Independence is highly valued in our land. We have a special day set aside to celebrate it! Yet we're not really independent. We may have gone beyond depending on our parents, but we don't grow our own food, pump our own water, manufacture our own cars and refine our own oil and produce our own electricity. We probably didn't build the house we live in or pave the street we drive on. We have armies and police to protect us from hostile people. We enjoy the freedoms we enjoy only because we have learned to work together, share our resources and talents and depend on one another in countless ways.

Jesus is telling us the more we learn to depend on

him, the more we remain united with him and draw life from him, then the more freedom we have from those forces that seek to enslave us: sin, addiction and hopelessness. Even death cannot ultimately conquer us for Jesus is the way, the truth and the life. He will prune us sometimes, but only that we might bear fruit; fruit being the result of a virtuous life within us; results that will endure for eternity.

6th Sunday of Easter
May 21, 2006

INTRODUCTION – The issue in today's first reading (Acts 10, 25-26. 34-35. 44-48) is how the Apostles should deal with Gentiles who heard about Jesus and started to believe in him. Should they have equal status with the Jews who were the original followers of Christ? Should they be required to follow all the Jewish laws, circumcision, strict dietary laws, and special feast days?

God gave St. Peter the answer to this question in a most unusual way. While Peter was in prayer, God gave Peter a vision of many different birds and animals. Many of them were birds and animals the Jews were not allowed to eat, such as pork. God told Peter to eat them. Peter said he would never eat anything forbidden. God said to him: "What God has made clean, you are not to call unclean." God had to say this three times to Peter, showing how difficult it was for Peter to grasp this idea. When the vision disappeared, God told Peter there were some men coming to see him and he was to go with them to the home of a Gentile named Cornelius, a Roman centurion. A strict Jew was not allowed to enter a Gentile's house, but God told him to, so he did. When

Peter got there he spoke to Cornelius and his relatives and friends about Jesus. As Peter finished speaking, Cornelius and all who were with him were filled with the Holy Spirit. This event is the background for today's first reading. Peter's entire speech is not included in the reading. The liturgy wants to get right to the point: that God's love in Jesus is meant for all people. Peter had finally understood what God had told him in his vision and without requiring these pagans to be circumcised or requiring them to accept Jewish traditions and customs, he ordered them all to be baptized.

HOMILY – Today's gospel (Jn 15, 9-17) has a great deal of meaning for me. When I was first ordained, I was teaching six hours a day at a high school and was assistant at one of the largest parishes in the city. Without trying to sound like a hero, I have to tell you I was a young priest, full of enthusiasm for my calling and I was busy all week except for a few hours I took off after school and parish duties on Friday evening. One day while I was praying, I heard in my heart our Lord speaking to me the words we just heard in the gospel: "I no longer call you slaves,...I have called you friends." I immediately knew he was telling me he wanted me to spend more than a couple of minutes in quiet prayer with him every day. In asking this he was asking for a little more friendship, a little more love. It wasn't a big deal he was asking of me, just that I work about 15 minutes less so I could spend 15 minutes more in prayer. I couldn't refuse his request when he put it that way: "I no longer call you slaves... I have called you friends." And so, I started spending a little more time in quiet prayer. And because I did that, and continue to do so, I have received so many blessings.

We know of course that real love shows itself more by what we do, than by what we say. But I'm sure we've seen situations where spouses or parents did lots of things for the family, but never had time to share themselves. I've known many a marriage that broke up just for that reason. They did things for each other but they never had time just to be with each other and share themselves with each other.

God could easily have created robots to do the things he wanted done. But he created people with hearts capable of love and he waits for us to love him. St. John tells us in today's second reading: "in this is love, not that we have loved God but that he loved us and sent his son as an expiation for our sins." (1 Jn 4, 7-10) And in his love he waits for our response. We are reminded of that love each time we come to Mass, each time we recall his death for us, each time he gives himself to us in the Eucharist.

Each time we come to the Eucharist we must remember that we are not only united with God in love, but we are united with one another. And so our Lord tells us twice in today's gospel to love one another. He tells us this is a commandment. It's interesting Jesus calls it a "commandment!" Many people today have a distorted notion of love. Too often we've seen people on TV or in the movies passionately saying to each other: "I love you." We tend to think love means romance and passion. It's something that flows out of us naturally and effortlessly. Now, I'm not against that kind of love. It's wonderful – it's even a preview of the love and joy we will experience in heaven. But if the divorce rate tells us anything, real love has to be more than passion. Love is not always dreamy and wonderful. Sometimes it's hard, sometimes it's less than exciting. Sometimes we have to be a loving person even when we don't feel like it and so Jesus said it is a commandment. Love means staying up with a sick child at times, forgiving a spouse who may have been insensitive, not getting our way all the time, taking time to communicate, being grateful for small favors. I got up this morning. I didn't feel like doing that. I would rather have stayed in bed. But I did it because of love, because I love God, I love you, the people I serve. Love isn't always warm fuzzy feelings, anyone who is married more than a couple of years knows it is a sense of commitment and dedication. The warm fuzzy feelings come and go. As today's gospel puts it, loving one another is a command, but Jesus gives us this command "so that my joy may be in you and your joy might be complete." You want more joy, ask the Lord to help you to lead you to greater love.

Our Lord, who is love itself as St. John tells us in today's second reading, has tried to teach us what is important for a love that will last. And what he has taught us is we must remain in him, for he will lead us to a love that cannot fail and a joy that is eternal.

Feast of the Ascension
May 28, 2006

(Acts 1: 1-11; Ephesians 4, 1-13; Mark 16, 15-20) Today we celebrate the feast of the Ascension. It is interesting to compare the way it is described in different parts of the Scriptures according to the particular purpose of each of the writers. St. Matthew, for example, doesn't describe the ascension at all. He implies there was a time when Jesus parted from them, and this parting seems to have taken place in Galilee. Matthew doesn't want to stress the parting so much as the idea that even though we can no longer see our Lord he is still with us. Jesus' last words in Matthew's gospel are: "Behold, I am with you always..." St. Luke, on the other hand, has Jesus leaving from Bethany, outside Jerusalem. There's even a rock there with a faint footprint on it which the tour guide will tell you is the very rock Jesus was standing on when he ascended. Luke gave us both the gospel of Luke and the Acts of the Apostles. In the Acts of the Apostles he tells us Jesus ascended 40 days after Easter. In his gospel we get the impression this happened on Easter Sunday. Today's gospel was from St. Mark's 16th chapter. If we read the entire 16th chapter of St. Mark, we also get the impression this event happened on Easter Sunday. St. Mark wants us to know that Jesus continues to work in and through the Church and the apostles. St. John's gospel is especially interesting as John not only gives us the impression the ascension took place on Easter Sunday, but that Jesus also gave the apostles the Holy Spirit on Easter Sunday night. I'm sure you remember the gospel for the second Sunday of Easter which was from John, how John tells us Jesus appeared to his apostles on Easter Sunday evening, wished them peace, showed them his hands and his side, told them he was sending them as he had been sent, then immediately he breathed on them and said: "Receive the Holy Spirit." All of this leaves us confused. When did Jesus ascend? And from where?

The gospels are very exact as to when the resurrection occurred, on the first day of the week, early in the morning; and where it happened: in a borrowed tomb where Jesus was buried outside of Jerusalem. Archeologists are nearly certain that the tomb around which the Church of the Holy Sepulcher is built is the exact tomb where Jesus was buried.

With the Ascension, it's obviously not the day or the place that is so important but the meaning of the event. I want to mention three meanings. 1) Jesus' risen body entered into the world of the divine. He is no longer present among us in a way that our senses can perceive him. For brief moments he did make himself visible to some of his followers but that period of time ended shortly after the resurrection and perhaps that's where the idea of the 40 days after the resurrection came from. When I say he entered into the world of the divine, I do not mean he wasn't already divine, the Son of God, the second person of the Blessed Trinity. It's that his human body, which had all the limitations that our own bodies have in terms of getting hungry, tired, feeling pain, that human body of Jesus was glorified and is now taken over with the fullness of his divine nature. The recent DeVinci Code says boldly that Jesus was revered simply as a wise human teacher and was not acclaimed as divine until the time of Constantine, who lived over three hundred years after Christ. Dan Brown's so called history and theology is as fictitious as his characters. The gospels and letters of the Apostles that we hear each Sunday were written two hundred to two hundred and fifty years before Constantine. And they were accepted as a true and authentic representation of Jesus Christ. That's why they became the gospels the Christian community used and honored as opposed to other so called "gospels" that were written later. If they had not given us an honest picture of Jesus Christ, they would have been long forgotten rather than copied and read again and again. Getting back to the ascension, it brings to completion and perfection the resurrection. Jesus not only came back to life, but he returned to the Father who had sent him and to quote Paul in today's second reading, Jesus was seated at God's right hand, "far above every principality, authority, power, and dominion..." And yet, although he is glorified at the right hand of the Father, he continues to be with us, but in a new way. We now come to know him not by physical sight but by meeting him through prayer, the sacraments, the Scriptures and through each other.

The second meaning of the ascension is that Jesus' ascension is a preview of God's plans for each of us who are faithful to him. We hope to rise to glory with him and to enter into a new life with him some day. When we say in the creed "we look for the resurrection of the dead" that does not mean we will come back to life and then spend eternity wandering aimlessly throughout the universe. Our resurrection will allow our bodies to share in new life in union with Jesus in God's kingdom.

There is a third meaning for the ascension: it's up to us to keep his work going ("Go into the whole world and proclaim the gospel to every creature...") Today there are about a billion believers in Jesus. That was only because a handful of his followers shared their faith with others. It's up to us now. If we keep our faith a secret from everyone else, we will not be doing anyone a favor. We need to share it, we need to ask people to come with us to Church and share in what we do. And it has to come more from you than from me. If I say something about God or faith or going to Church, people will think "well, he's supposed to say that. That's what he's getting paid for." If you say it it will carry much more weight. "Go into the whole world and proclaim the gospel to every creature..." is meant for all those who believe in Jesus.

Summing things up: Christ is with us now as we gather in his name. He promised he would be, and he gives himself to us in the Eucharist. He gives us a preview of our own future glory in his ascension and he has left us with the job of continuing his work, bringing the message of faith and the love of God to others. Amen.

Pentecost
June 4, 2006

(Acts 2, 1-11; 1 Cor. 12, 3b-7. 12-13; John 20, 12-23) Pentecost is one of the three most important feasts of the Church year. We know Christmas is one of the three. It's easy to get excited about the birth of a baby, especially when the baby is God's Son and his mother is the Virgin Mary. We know the feast of Jesus' resurrection is the most important feast of all, because if there were no resurrection, we would have no faith or hope at all. But Pentecost, the third most important feast, seems like another ordinary Sunday.

Let me give you a little history of Pentecost. It was not invented by the Church. The Jews were celebrating Pentecost 3000 years ago. It was one of their three most important feasts. It was originally a harvest feast on which the first fruits were offered in gratitude to God. It later came to be celebrated as the anniversary of the giving of the Law to Moses on Mt. Sinai. The word itself means simply 50th, the 50th day after Jewish Passover. The Jews were celebrating that feast when the Spirit came on Jesus' followers. And so Pentecost is still celebrated, but we who are Christians celebrate it as the day on which God sent his Holy Spirit upon the Church.

Pentecost isn't just the celebration of a past event. It is important for us today, because the Holy Spirit is important for us today. The Spirit is hard to picture because the Spirit is within us when we are in God's grace. The Spirit is like the air we breathe, the light that goes on when we have an idea, the fire that burns in our heart. And so the Scriptures use these symbols help us know the Spirit; in the first reading the Spirit is a strong driving wind whereas in John's gospel the

Spirit is the gentle breath of Jesus who breathes on his apostles and says "Receive the Holy Spirit." In either case, whether as a powerful wind or a gentle breath, the Spirit is like the invisible air we cannot live without. The Spirit is like the light that goes on in our mind when we have an idea: Jesus tells us in the gospel "he will guide you to all truth." Jesus couldn't explain everything to the apostles that he wanted them to know, but the Spirit turned on the light in their minds to be able to understand all that he had been teaching them. The Spirit also appeared to the apostles as tongues of fire, a fire that started burning in them to proclaim Christ with courage and conviction.

God wants us to know him and love him and the Spirit helps us to do that. But because the Spirit works within us, we are not aware the Spirit is even there. I would like to share with you some thoughts from C.S. Lewis about how we grow in knowledge things, people and God. If we want to know something about rocks, for example, we go and we find rocks. They won't come to us, they won't run away from us. In no way do they cooperate with us in getting to know them. The initiative is all on our side if we are to know rocks. If we want to study wild animals, that's a little different. We have to go find them and if we're not really quiet they probably will run away from us (or eat us alive). The initiative is mostly on our part if we are to know about wild animals, but they could prevent us from knowing them. If we want to know another human being, and they are determined for us not to know them, we probably won't. We have to win their confidence if they are going to open up to us. The initiative is equally divided: it takes two to make a friendship. When it comes to God, there is no way we could find him or know him if he didn't show himself to us. And he has done so in Jesus Christ. But we cannot not know Jesus Christ without the help of the Spirit. As Paul tells us in today's second reading: "No one can say Jesus is Lord except in the Holy Spirit." Without the Spirit God is totally unknown to us. The Spirit makes the Scriptures alive for us and helps us to be aware of God's presence with us and God's love for us.

When we have this kind of a relationship with God it spills over into everything else we do. So St. Paul tells us in Galatians: if we live by the Spirit, the Spirit will produce in us love, joy, peace, patience, kindness, goodness, faithfulness, humility, and self-control." Most of us also are familiar with Paul's description of the greatest gift of the Spirit: "I may be able to speak the languages of men and even angels, but if have not love, my speech is no more than a noisy gong or a clanging bell...Love is patient and kind, love is not jealous, etc, etc.

One last point: it was on the Church, that God sent his Spirit. As the first reading tells us Christ followers were all together in one place. The Spirit gives different gifts to different members of the Church so we can help each other to know and experience God and God's love. If we want to experience the fullness of the Spirit, we need each other, we need to come together, to worship together, to share our gifts with one another. Without the Spirit we are trying to breathe without air, think without light, love without fire.

Trinity Sunday
June 11th 2006

INTRODUCTION – (Dt. 4, 32-34. 39-40; Romans 8, 14-17; Matthew 28, 16-20) It's only in modern times that people started doubting the existence of God. In the thousands of years human beings have lived on this planet, the tendency has been just the opposite, people have usually worshipped a multiplicity of gods, with only one exception that I know of. There was a pharaoh in Egypt about 1375 years B.C., Akhnaton, who decreed that only the sun god, Aton, could be publicly worshipped in Egypt. Ten years after he died, the famous King Tut reinstated all the gods the people previously venerated. The Romans had gods whose names are still familiar to us: Mercury, Venus, Mars, Jupiter, Neptune and Pluto. The people of Israel were unique among all the nations. They had only one God, the God who revealed himself to Abraham over 1800 years before Christ. But they were not always faithful to their God, and were often seduced by the decadent worship of their pagan neighbors. In today's first reading we hear Moses declare that there is no other God than the Lord and that only by being faithful to their God will they prosper. It's still good advice for today's world where polytheism and paganism have been replaced by atheism, hedonism and materialism.

HOMILY – Today is Father's Day and I congratulate all fathers here today. A recent Gallup Poll identifies the most significant family problem facing America today is the absence of fathers in the home. Almost half of America's children grow up without a father at home. We don't realize how devastating this is to our society. Most people in poverty are young single mothers. And the odds are high that more children from fatherless homes will get into trouble. 60% of rapists, 72% of adolescent murderers and 70% of our country's long-term prison population are from fatherless homes. When fathers are absent from homes, boys tend to be more violent and girls tend to become more sexually active. And this early sexual activity only contributes to a ever worsening vicious circle. Even in families where there is a father, there are those who think their only role is to bring home the paycheck and that it's the mother's job to raise the children. According to the US Census, fathers who are at home tend to spend only about 20 minutes a day with their children. I am quoting all of these statistics not to make people feel guilty, but to tell dads you are vitally important to the well being of your family.

Today's first reading is telling us the same thing today with regard to our Father in heaven. Moses told the people that they must be faithful to their God that they and their children may prosper. When the people abandoned their God, they lost the light that gave them guidance and wisdom and the power that gave them strength as a nation.

Jesus even more clearly revealed God to us as our father. That's the way he taught us to pray. Many times when I pray, I just dwell on those two words. God is our Father. He belongs to us, he belongs to me. I can call on him and know he is there and he is listening. He doesn't always do what I want him to do. That wouldn't be a good way for any father to raise a child, to do everything for his child or to give his child everything his child wanted.

I think of the example of a father teaching his child how to build a bird house. The father could do it much more easily himself, but he wants his child to learn and so he patiently holds back while the child hammers and saws and probably makes a few mistakes. Life is much more complicated than building a bird house, but I am sure God could do lots of things much more easily than waiting for us to do them, but he tends to patiently hold back so we can learn, even as we make a few mistakes along the way. So many times when I call on my Father in heaven, he says to me "I could do that for you, but I wouldn't be helping you if I did. There's something here you need to learn."

As I talk about the Father today, I cannot ignore Jesus and the Holy Spirit, because today is Trinity Sunday. This Sunday touches the basic mystery behind all the other mysteries of our faith. The Father sent his Son to save us by his life, his teachings, his miracles, his death and resurrection. And the Father and the Son sent us the Holy Spirit to fill us with divine life, to make us truly God's children. Today at Mass as always we honor our Father, through Jesus his Son in unity with the Holy Spirit. Does this puzzle us that there is a Father and a Son and a Holy Spirit, three distinct persons yet only one God? Of course it does. But it should not surprise us that we cannot fully understand God. Sometimes we think we're so smart, but the things we know are like a pebble on the beach compared to all the things that are still a mystery to us, even in the material universe of which we are a part. So we shouldn't be surprised that the One who created of all these things is too much for us to fully understand.

And if you think that the Trinity is a mystery, there is an even bigger one to try to fathom. Why? Why would God bother about us? Why would God invite us to share in his own life? For the same reason a mother or father will sacrifice themselves for their child. There's only one answer to the question: Why? Because God is a Father, a Father who is love.

The Body and Blood of Christ
June 18th 2006

(Exodus 24, 3-8; Hebrews 9, 11-15; Mark 14, 12-16. 22-26) I wonder how many people here have ever seen the Vitamin A in a carrot, the Vitamin C in an orange or the potassium in a banana. I've seen lots of vitamin *pills*, but I wouldn't know what an actual vitamin molecule looked like even if it came up and bit me. Yet the experts tell us they *are* in certain foods whether we can see them or not. With this thought in mind we could make a simple comparison with the Eucharist, in so far as we cannot see Christ present in the Eucharist; but it doesn't matter that we can't see him, he is still there. I would like to extend this comparison a bit further. Health experts tell us that without the sufficient amounts of vitamins, minerals, carbohydrates, proteins and fats in our diet we will not be healthy and we may even die. We are told to eat a variety of foods so that we get all the nutrients we need. We tend not to question the health experts that tell us all of this. We trust they know what they are talking about. Even though there is probably no one here who follows their recommendations perfectly, I think many Americans are beginning to pay attention to following a good diet, especially as some of us get older. But there are also many who seem to think that those who promote good nutrition are just trying to take all the fun out of life and so they go their merry way filling themselves full of saturated fats, salt, sugar, nicotine and alcohol. The experts who tell us how to take care of ourselves can't help us much if we don't believe them or follow the suggestions they give us.

Today's feast puts us in touch with another expert, Jesus. He tells us what we need to do to be healthy spiritually. How do we know he is an expert we should listen to. Well, he told us he knows what he is talking about, but he also knows many will not believe him just because he said so. So, he told us if we are not sure we want to believe him, to look at his works. "If I do not perform my Father's works, do not believe me; but if I perform them, even if you do not believe me, believe the works, so that you may realize that the Father is in me and I am in the Father." (Jn 11,37-38) Of course we were not there personally to see the miracles Jesus worked, but there were many who did witness his works and there were those who gave their lives as a testimony that what they preached about Jesus was true. So if we decide to believe the words of those who saw him and knew him and who died for him, then we can only conclude that when he speaks to us about things that are beyond us we ought to listen to what he had to say. And if we listen to what he had to say, we will discover that he has a few things to say about nutrition too. He doesn't tell us about the vitamins and minerals we need to keep our physical lives healthy though. He has a much greater purpose in mind. He tells us, "I came that they may have life and may have it to the full." (Jn 10,10) And the food that will nourish that life is himself. For he tells us "I am the bread of life." (Jn 6,35) "Whoever eats this bread will live forever." (Jn 6,58) Now that's the ultimate healthy diet. Today's gospel tells us how he becomes our food.

If many of us have difficulty trusting and especially if we have difficulty following the research and expertise of those who advocate eating a well balanced and healthy diet, then I suppose it's not too great of a surprise that many have difficulty trusting and especially following the guidance of Jesus who is our expert on eternal life. We see a great number of people, even Catholics, who try to tells us Jesus didn't really mean what he said when he said "This is my body.". They tell us its all symbolism. Long before the Last Supper, many of Jesus' followers walked away from him shaking their heads in disbelief when he said to them "Amen, amen, I say to you, unless you eat the flesh of the Son of Man and drink his blood you do not have life within you." (Jn 6,53) When he saw them walk away, he didn't call them back and say "Heh! Come back, you misunderstood me." He knew they were leaving him because they *did* understand what he said to them. At that point, he just turned to his apostles and asked "Do you also want to leave?" (Jn 6,67) Jesus is our expert on eternal life and he tells us the food he offers us, which is himself, will nourish us forever. Today's feast challenges our belief in him and in his presence with us in the Eucharist.

There was a time in history when so few people were being fed by the Eucharist that the Church had to make a *law* saying that Catholics were obliged to receive Communion at least once a year. Even up to 40 or 50 years ago, people went to Communion very seldom. There was a heresy at that time called Jansenism which told people they were unworthy to receive Communion unless they went to confession first. The Eucharist was held in such *high* respect that people stayed away. Now many people have lost their belief in Christ's presence in the Eucharist, and consequently they stay away too. They stay away in the sense that its too much trouble to come to Mass. It seems to me as if the devil tries every trick he can to keep people away from Communion. Either the devil tells us it is so sacred we shouldn't receive it, or he tells us there's nothing worth going there for anyway.

The real crisis of faith in the Catholic Church at the

present time I think has its origin right here in the mystery we celebrate today. There are many who no longer believe that the Eucharist is really and truly the body and blood of Jesus Christ. I think this lack of belief is connected with the vocation crisis. I think it's the reason Mass attendance has dropped off. And then, like a domino effect, when people get away from church and Mass attendance, they are getting away from their spiritual roots. Without a strong spiritual foundation to build our lives on, we are left with fewer values to live by and fewer values to pass on to our children. Do I overemphasize the importance of the Eucharist? I don't think so. Certainly God's love is shown to us in many ways, but I believe the Eucharist helps us to see those ways more clearly in which God's love is present in our lives and I believe it is also the Eucharist itself, more than anything else, that tells us that God loves us and that God is with us.

12th Sunday in Ordinary Time
June 25, 2006

(Job 38, 1. 8-11; 2 Cor. 5, 14-17; Mark 4, 35-41) Four hunters were out tramping through the woods looking for deer. Suddenly a large buck jumped out of the bushes and they all fired at once. The deer fell down dead, but when they examined it it was only hit by one bullet. They couldn't' figure out whose bullet had killed the deer and while they were arguing over it a game warden came by. They asked him to help them figure out who brought down the deer. After examining it he asked whether there was a preacher in the group. One of the men said he was and the game warden said the deer was his. They were amazed at his answer and asked how he had figured that out. The game warden said, well the deer was killed with only one bullet and it went in one ear and out the other.

God did not reveal the concept of reward and punishment, heaven and hell, in the next life until about a century or two before the time of Christ. Prior to that time they thought that when a person died, the soul went to a place somewhere down below the surface of the earth called Sheol. Sheol was a place where nothing much ever happened. The spirit of a person experienced neither happiness nor unhappiness there. At the same time, God's people firmly believed that God was just and fair, that God rewarded good people and punished bad people. Because they had no clue that reward or punishment could occur *after* this life, they logically concluded that, since God is fair, God rewards us in this life if we're good or punishes us in this life if we're bad. The logical conclusion to that kind of theology is that if we look at a person and see they are prosperous, healthy, happy, and blessed in numerous ways, that is a sign they are a really virtuous and holy person. Conversely, if a person is having problems, if they are poor, or suffer from physical sickness, or suffer in some other way, they must be being punished for some evil in their life, even if they themselves are unaware of anything evil they might have done.

But they were smart enough to know things didn't always work that way. Sometimes bad things happened to good people while other people got away with murder. These everyday realities must have caused a real crisis of faith for many good people at that time. The book of Job tries to explore this dilemma. Job is a very holy and good man. Even God admits it at the beginning of the book. He is blessed in every way. But by a few sudden tragedies he loses his crops, his livestock, his lands, the respect of his peers, and all of his sons and daughters. His wife and a few faithful friends kept telling him he must deserve all this for something he did. Most of us are familiar with his initial view of what was happening to him when he declared: "the Lord gives and the Lord takes away." People often speak of the "patience of Job," but even his patience wore thin and he started asking for answers, or rather I should say he started demanding answers as to why he was suffering all these things.

God's response to his demands came in the form of questions, questions mostly about the mysteries of nature, questions like we hear in today's first reading such as "who has power over the sea and the waves." These questions go on for four chapters as God asks Job how the stars were put in place, how the clouds are formed, what causes the wind to blow, who feeds the fish in the depths of the sea, or how do the animals in the wild live. These questions were meant to lead the readers of the book of Job to a sense of trust that God is in control of all things. Even if we don't understand or know what he's doing, he knows, and we just have to trust him.

Through the life, death and resurrection of Jesus we have been given more insights, more answers, more help to our faith and to the mystery of suffering than Job was able to come up with. And yet, many of us still tend to think about life the way that people long before Jesus did. At least subconsciously we think if we are good, God should make life pleasant for us and if other people are bad (not us of course!) God should not let them get by with it. Sometimes that's the way things happen. A good life does have many rewards and an evil life usually catches up with a person, but it doesn't <u>always</u> happen right away. And when life doesn't go the way we think it should, our faith is shaken. We don't understand how

God works. We are somewhat like the apostles in today's gospel, when storms come up we cry out, "Lord, don't you care that we are going to drown?"

In each Sunday's liturgy, in Communion, in our prayers, God gives us as many answers as he thinks we can understand right now. We have the good news that God loves us so much that he sent his only Son to teach us, to heal us and to suffer and die for us. We have the resurrection which gives us hope that sin and evil and suffering will not have the last word. We have the Eucharist which tells us that in our journey through life God will not abandon us, but will always be with us to strengthen us and unite us closely with himself. The answers we get, like the answers Job got, continue to require us to have faith. Jesus asked the apostles in today's gospel, "Why are you so terrified? Why are you so lacking in faith?" Jesus asks us those same questions today. As I meditated on this gospel, I wondered how the apostles might have responded if Jesus had asked those questions before he calmed the storm. Think about that for a moment. If he did, do you think they would have heard him? It probably would have gone in one ear and out the other as they would have been too worried about the storm. It's easy for anyone to see we should have trusted more after danger has past, but our Lord wants us to hear this question also when the storm is raging and the waves are high. God wants us to know he is still in control, even though we may wonder, "how can he be?"

13th Sunday in Ordinary Time
July 2, 2006

INTRODUCTION – The first reading (Wisdom 1, 13-15, 2,23-24) tells us God did not make death. Rather, it came about through the envy of the devil. This is obviously a commentary on the story of Adam and Eve in the garden – how they tried to find their happiness and fulfillment by doing things their way rather than God's way. They didn't trust what God told them. When the devil convinces us not to live the way God tells us we need to live in order to find happiness, we find death. The two miracles in today's gospel show us what can happen to people who put their trust in Jesus. The second reading is an appeal to the Corinthians (2 Cor. 8, 7. 9. 13-15) for financial help for the poor in Jerusalem.

HOMILY – I love the Irish story of Fr. Mc Kenzie who was called out late one night to go on a sick call. On his way he had to pass the local pub and as he looked in the window he saw some of his parishioners still sitting at the bar, drinking pretty heavily. He felt it was his obligation to chastise them about being out so late. He walked in the door and called out to the first one: "Sullivan, do you want to go to heaven?" Sullivan answered "yes, Father." So Father said "well, get off that bar stool and get over here." And Sullivan obediently came to where Father told him. Then he called to the next one: "Kelly, do you want to go to heaven?" Kelly answered, "yes, Father." And Father Mc Kenzie said "Well, you get over here too." And Kelly came. Then Father said to Murphy: "Murphy, do you want to go to heaven?" "Indeed I do Father." Father said, "Well, then get away from that bar and come over here." Murphy said "No, I'm not going to do that!" Father said:

"Murphy, don't you want to go to heaven when you die."
Murphy said, "oh, yes, Father, when I die, but I thought
you were getting ready to go right now."

We all want to go to heaven some day, but none of
us are in a hurry to get there. But indeed, some day we
will die. There was a man who was a workaholic. And
he paid a high price for his fanatic dedication to his job.
He got to the point where his relationship with his
family was suffering where he was nervous and irritable,
had high blood pressure, couldn't sleep and was in
general falling apart. He went to see the doctor along
with his wife. The doctor told him that he was
physically exhausted and he had to get some rest or he
wouldn't survive. He prescribed six months away from
work and total rest at home. The doctor then wanted to
talk with the man's wife, alone. He told her that her
husband was critically ill and his recovery depended on
her. She had to see that he got all the rest he could, not
to argue with him, wait on him as much as possible and
make life as peaceful and pleasant as she could. If she
didn't her husband was going to die. On the way home
the husband asked his wife "What did the doctor have
to tell you?" She answered him, "The doctor said you
were going to die."

So are we all, but hopefully not in the near future.
We may make jokes about death, but we can't take it
lightly. Our eternal happiness depends on whether we
are ready to meet our God when the time comes. So as
unpleasant a thought as it may be, we have to always
keep it in mind so we are prepared for it when it comes.
God didn't create us to live in this world forever. He
created us to live with him forever in eternal life. Our
readings today speak of these profound truths. Our first
reading today tells us God did not make death. God

formed us to be imperishable, in God's own image and likeness, but it was though the devil that death came into this world. This is obviously a theological reflection on the first few chapters of Genesis.

Jesus, in today's gospel, (Mk. 5, 21-43), shows too that he has power of life and death and that his mission was to bring life to us. The life he gave to the little girl was a dramatic and visible sign of what he wishes to give us in an invisible realm, for the little girl would eventually grow up and die a natural death, but the life he wishes for us is eternal. There is a quote from John's gospel which I love where Jesus says this explicitly: "I came that they may have life and may have it abundantly (i.e. to an extent that is overflowing)." (Jn. 10, 10) We don't know what that might be like, but we have a sense of it in Jesus' resurrection. Heaven will be a sharing in his risen life, which is of course a sharing in God's own life. Pain and suffering will no longer exist, which today's gospel also tells us. That life will be characterized by peace and love and joy.

Mark is showing us in today's gospel that the way to this life is through faith, not a dead faith which only says "I believe" but a living faith that we put into action. Notice Jesus said to the woman he healed "daughter, your faith has saved you." And he said to the synagogue official, Jairus: "Do not be afraid, just have faith." Notice, the people who laughed at Jesus, i.e. those without faith, were put out of the house.

Our faith leads to hope without which we are hope-less. And there is no joy without hope. Joy is built on hope. And our faith also leads to love which St. Paul is talking about today, a love that reaches out to those who are not as richly blessed as we are. Amen.

14th Sunday in Ordinary Time
July 9, 2006

INTRODUCTION – (Ezekiel 2, 2-5; 2 Cor. 12, 7-10) Sometimes prophets predicted the future, but most of the time they tried to direct God's people to live by God's commands. Their efforts to do so were not always appreciated by the people. The prophet Ezekiel lived about 600 years before Christ, before, during and after the Babylonians destroyed Jerusalem. He had to warn the people of the destruction that was to come if they did not change their ways. We hear in today's first reading God's warning to Ezekiel that as a prophet he would not have an easy job of it. The passage prepares us for the gospel which tells of the cold reception Jesus received when he came to his hometown of Nazareth to preach.

HOMILY – (Mark 6, 1-6) We just heard about the reception Jesus received in his own hometown of Nazareth. His family and neighbors already heard stories about his teachings and his miracles. In St. Luke's gospel we are told there was some initial positive reaction to his teaching there, but something happened. Perhaps they rejected him because he came from the working class and was not educated as a rabbi. They asked: "Where did he get all this?" Perhaps he suffered the fate of all the other prophets who were rejected because the people didn't want to hear the message about keeping God's commandments and living a good life. We know from the gospels not everyone was negative toward him, but there were enough people who were that they were able to convince the others. The people were so negative, in fact, that St. Mark tells us that Jesus <u>was not able</u> to work any miracles there except for a few healings. A lack of faith actually

<u>prevents</u> God from helping us as he would like. St. Luke tells us that before his visit to Nazareth was over they wanted to kill him, but he got away.

It is a blessing that God has not lost patience with us or given up on all of us. He continues to try to send us people to teach us how to live good and holy lives in spite of our rebellious natures. It is a great honor for God to call someone to be his prophet, but it is also a difficult and often thankless task. You who are parents know what it's like. The job of a parent is not as prominent as that of an Ezekiel or Jeremiah or Jesus, but to a lesser degree a parent's role is the same as a prophet, trying to teach their children to be good and sometimes having to face a fair amount of resistance. I remember my dad would always quote the proverb from today's gospel: "A prophet is honored everywhere except in his own house." My dad was a CPA and he got paid for his advice. When he tried to tell us something at home, we never ignored him - that would have been like taking our life in our hands, but we didn't always jump to agree with him. So he would say "a prophet is not without honor...except in his own house." We always did what we were told (we didn't want to face the consequences if we didn't) but we didn't always want to do it. Parents, if they are good parents, have a difficult job at times, especially in today's society. It's so easy just to give in every time a child wants something. Children need to know their parents love them enough to do the hard job of trying to teach them what's right. Too many parents I have met argue: "Why fight it? The kids will do what they want." They will do what they want if they can get by with it. But if the parents don't guide them right, the child will be less likely to make good value judgments when they are on their own.

It's not just parents, however, who have the

prophetic role of helping others to know God and to know God's ways. In the sacrament of Confirmation we are all anointed to be witnesses of Christ and of our faith whenever the opportunity arises. Sometimes we can witness through words of encouragement, as long as we don't get too preachy. Sometimes we can witness by sharing with another person how much help our faith gives us. Sometimes we can only witness by our love, by a good life and by prayer.

There is one other aspect of our gospel we must not miss. God usually communicates with us in very simple ways. The people of Nazareth thought they couldn't learn anything from a carpenter. In our pride, our envy, our prejudices, our willingness to follow the crowd, we can easily miss the ways God is trying to break through our defenses. This morning/afternoon he comes to us in a most simple way: as food and drink. Yet for those who have eyes to see, in this holy meal it is infinite life and love that is given to us.

15th Sunday in Ordinary Time
July 16, 2006

INTRODUCTION – (Amos 7, 12-15; Ephesians 1, 3-14; Mark 6, 7-13) I said last week, before the reading from the prophet Ezekiel that sometimes prophets predicted the future but most of the time they tried to direct God's people to live by God's commands. Their efforts to do so were not always appreciated. Today in our first reading we hear from the prophet Amos who lived over 700 years before Christ. At that time in Israel there were people who made a career out of being prophets. Whether called by God or not, they would speak for God, telling people how to solve their problems, giving them advice, predict the future, etc., *all for an appropriate fee.* You can imagine that these professional prophets would tend not to be offensive people or say anything that could possibly be upsetting or they might not get paid. As he says in today's first reading, the prophet Amos was not one of these professionals. He was a farmer but God called him to go to Bethel, a major city in Israel, to confront the people about their sinful lives and to warn them their immoral living would lead to their destruction. His blunt and honest message did not make people happy, and the high priest there told him to "get out of town." Today's passage prepares the way for the gospel where Jesus sends his apostles out to preach and warns them they may not always be welcome.

HOMILY – When my classmate, Fr. Jerry Bensman, and I go away for vacation, you should see our car. It is loaded down with stuff: suitcases, Mass kit, things to read, video and audio tapes, backgammon board, food, etc. About sixteen years ago I went on a three-month study program to Greece, Turkey, Egypt and Israel. All I was allowed to take with me was one suitcase and one small carry- on case. It was a challenge to get all the things I would need for three months into those two pieces of luggage, but I managed. I never ran out of anything except money. *(This is off the subject.)* I saw a doctor over there, and if you think medical expenses are bad here in the U.S., you should see what they charge in Israel. But it wasn't just medical expenses that were sky high. The doctor told me that 70% of his fee was taken by the government as taxes. All that's besides the point I want to make though. My point is that for three months I was quite comfortable with just the few items I was able to bring with me. It's amazing how much stuff we <u>think</u> we need.

In today's gospel Jesus is sending his apostles out to do some preaching and healing. They are told to travel light. He allows them to wear sandals and have a walking stick (in St. Matthew's gospel they were not even allowed to have those things.) They were not allowed to take money or food or an extra change of clothes. Probably they were not traveling very far or wouldn't be gone for very long, but even then they had to depend on people's hospitality and on God's providence for everything they needed. I don't think the Lord expects everyone to live in such simplicity and poverty, although there have been holy people who managed to do so, such as St. Francis or Mother Theresa. I think our Lord is telling us we don't have to have a lot of things to survive or even to be comfortable and happy. In other words, "travel light" is one of the messages from today's gospel.

Sometimes we forget that as we go through life we're just tourists visiting this planet; we're on a long trip but we're not staying here forever. As St. Paul tells us, our destination, our real home is heaven. We're not going to take anything with us there, except our good deeds. How about all the stuff we're dragging with us through life; is it helping us move forward to our final goal or is it slowing us down, or even worse, is it a distraction that makes us forget where we're going? Sometimes it's the quest for material things that loads us down on this journey, but it can be other things too. Sports can hold such a priority in people's lives that they never have time to pray or get to church on Sunday or to spend quality time with their family. An excessive love for entertainment or always being too busy can do the same thing. Maybe it's a lot of anger and resentment that we keep holding on to, or addictions and bad habits. St. Paul tells us that God chose us before the world began to be holy and blameless in his sight. If we were created to be holy, what is getting in our way? The stuff that slows us down in our journey to God can also keep us from finding true joy as we go through life. It will limit our experience of the Lord who is our ultimate peace and joy. May I end with a simple example? If we try to swim with too much weighing us down, we do not do well. We may be so weighted down that we just sink. It's possible for a person to let so many things get in the way of their relationship with God that they sink spiritually too.

16th Sunday in Ordinary Time
July 23, 2006

INTRODUCTION – (Jeremiah, 23, 1-6; Ephesians, 2, 13-18; Mk. 6, 30-34) (*I used the following as introduction to the penitential rite*): In the Scriptures, those who were leaders of God's people: kings and priests, teachers and other spiritual leaders were often compared to shepherds. Frequently these leaders were more interested in serving themselves than they were in providing good leadership for God's people. Jeremiah, today's first reading, blames the kings of Judah for the destruction of the nation under the Babylonians. In today's gospel our Lord views the people of his day as sheep without a shepherd and has compassion on them. He is a good shepherd. He desires to lead his followers to glory and eternal happiness. The way to follow him is through faith and love. For the times we have failed, we ask his forgiveness and his help to do better.

HOMILY – Last Sunday's gospel ended with Jesus sending his apostles out to neighboring towns to preach repentance and to heal the sick and drive out demons. Today's gospel begins with their return. They had much to tell Jesus. They must have been excited to have been able to do some of the same wonderful works they had seen Jesus do. But they were also worn out. Jesus said, "you need to rest," but they weren't getting any rest where they were as so many people sought their ministry. Their escape from the crowd proved to be unsuccessful.

Two thoughts struck me that deserve further reflection. (1) Jesus told his apostles, "come away by yourselves to a deserted place and rest a while." The need for rest is something most of us can relate to. There is so little time and so much to do for most of us. Yet we need time to rest! There is even a law telling us to do so. The law says: "Keep holy the Lord's day." We usually think that means go to church on Sunday (or Saturday night) and it does. But originally it also allowed people to take a day off. That commandment began as a gift to the Israelites who had just escaped from slavery. It told them they didn't have to work seven days a week as they had to do as slaves. They were no one's property. They were free to take a day off and no one would punish them. They would give some of that day to God who created them and had done so much for them and the rest they could spend with their families. This is one of the things that has made Jewish families so strong. Jesus did not annul those ten laws God gave Moses. He wants us to continue enjoying this gift he gave to the Jews. I would like you to notice in today's gospel when Jesus said to the apostles: "Come away..." He was inviting them to take some time to relax *with him.* We do that when we come to Mass. We stop our busy-ness for about an hour and we spend it with him. Sometimes I see people yawning at Mass or during the sermon. They get embarrassed if they know

I saw them. I've said before that doesn't bother me. Prayer is very relaxing and if we haven't had enough sleep, we start to yawn. I just hope you don't relax so much I lose you! When you leave here and go home, I have one word of caution. Watch out for the TV. Good programs can re-create us and inspire us, but much of the stuff on TV does for our mind what junk food does for our body. It satisfies us momentarily but doesn't provide any real nourishment. And be careful not to let the TV or internet take over our lives or isolate us from our families (which happens in some homes).

(2) Notice our Lord didn't ask his apostles to teach the crowd. Jesus alone was the teacher. They didn't know enough yet to teach. They were being trained to heal people and cast our demons and they could preach that people must repent of their sins. They wouldn't be ready to teach until the Holy Spirit came upon them. We need to reflect that Jesus helped people not only by healing them but by teaching them. The Catholic Church continues Jesus' ministry of teaching in a variety of ways, not least of which is the Catholic School system. But our learning about God and about Jesus Christ does not end the day we leave the Catholic School. What we learned about our faith in school was just a little bit, because it was all we could absorb at the time. We can recall what the poet Alexander Pope said: "A little learning is a dangerous thing." The danger is that we assume we know enough about our faith. St. John of the Cross tells us no matter how many mysteries and wonders we come to understand about God, "...the greater part still remains to be ...understood..." God is infinite and God's love is infinite. This is another good reason to come to Mass every Sunday and also a good reason to spend time reading the Scriptures. It is normal for people who follow Christ to consider

themselves disciples of Christ. If you look up the word "disciple" in the dictionary, you will find it comes from the Latin word *dicere* which means "to learn." If we think we no longer need to learn any more about God and about Jesus Christ, then we should no longer call ourselves disciples. For with Christ we are always in the process of learning.

17th Sunday in Ordinary Time
July 30, 2006

(2 Kings 4, 42-44; Ephesians 4, 1-6; John 6, 1-15) Our gospel readings for most of this year are from St. Mark. In our reading from St. Mark so far we have come to the part where he tells us about Jesus miraculously feeding a great crowd with only a few loaves of bread and a couple of fish. St. Mark's gospel is the shortest of the four gospels, and if we stayed with Mark all thru the year we would run out of gospels before the year ended. So as we come to the account of the multiplication of the loaves, we shift into St. John's version of the miracle, (chapter 6) which is, I believe, one of the most beautiful chapters in all four gospels. St. John expands on this event at much greater length and sees in this miracle a preview of the Eucharist.

All of the miracles of Jesus were spectacular, especially raising people from the dead. We hear about different ones in the different gospels, but this is the only one, other than the resurrection of Jesus, that all four gospels tell us about. It must have been truly inspiring and impressive.

We will continue hearing from this wonderful 6th chapter of St. John all next month, with the exception of the Transfiguration next Sunday, and we will see the obvious connection of this miracle with the Eucharist. We see a hint of this even in today's gospel when, as St. John describes it, Jesus took the loaves, gave thanks and distributed them. The Greek verb for "gave thanks" is ευχαριστέω. You might notice too, after the people were fed, little is said about the fish. All the focus from now on is on the loaves of bread.

I could point out about a dozen different thoughts from today's gospel that would merit our reflection, but I will restrict myself to only two points. As we hear the account, we might notice what could be a small miracle within the larger one. The small miracle I am thinking of is the act of generosity on the part of the little boy. We presume, from the mention of barley loaves, that he was poor as that was the bread of the poor. He could have thought to himself: "I can't really help anyone with the little food I have. I'll just keep it for myself." But he didn't think that way. He was willing to offer what he had to help feed a few other people. Then the big miracle came. Jesus fed everyone with his small offering of five barley loaves and two fish.

Perhaps Jesus asks us at times to give him something that seems small and insignificant. Maybe our Lord asks us to give 5 or 10 minutes a day in prayer and we say to ourselves, "that's hardly worth doing. I probably should say a rosary every day." Which, of course, we never get around to doing, but we never get around to spending an extra 5 or 10 minutes in prayer either because it seems so small. Or he asks us to give a couple of extra dollars to the poor and we think, "there are so many poor people how can I help?" We do nothing because we're overwhelmed. Or maybe he asks us to give a little of our talent, join the choir or even sing in church and we think our voice isn't that good, so we don't do anything. The Lord can and will work miracles with what we're willing to trust him with.

My second point: At the conclusion of today's gospel, we hear that the people were so impressed that they wanted to make Jesus king. Jesus saw right through that. They wanted somebody who would take care of them, not just by providing them with free meals, but someone who would give them back their own nation, their own government. The Jews were tired of Roman oppression and they figured Jesus could get enough of a following to revolt. Wanting to have a free lunch or even their own independence wasn't all bad, but Jesus was at a different place than they were at. His intentions were much more wonderful than the people could ever imagine. Jesus came to feed his people with spiritual food, food that would sustain them not for a day or even for a lifetime, but for eternity. He wanted to set them free, not so much from the Romans, but from every other power that seeks to oppress and destroy us: death, sickness, hatred, prejudice, injustice. They were hungry for what they <u>imagined</u> they needed rather than being hungry for what God <u>knew </u>they needed. He withdrew from them to the mountain, alone, but only for a short time. It ended up, as we will hear, <u>they</u> withdrew from <u>him</u> because they really didn't want, or really didn't believe in, what he had to give. It still happens today; God may temporarily seem to withdraw from us because he doesn't do what we want. And we continue to withdraw from him because we don't want what he desires to give us.

One last thought. The Eucharist is the way Christ chose to continue feeding his people with a miraculous food, his own flesh and blood. We will hear him say in three weeks: "Unless you eat the flesh of the son of man and drink his blood you do not have life in you." We gather here today in faith in obedience to his words at the Last Supper: "Take this and eat...take this and drink...do this in memory of me." May we experience his presence with us now as he feeds us in a miraculous way with his own body and blood. Amen.

Transfiguration
August 6, 2006

INTRODUCTION – Our first reading is from the book of Daniel (Dn. 7, 7-10.13-14). The author of this book lived during the time the Greeks dominated most of the known world. The Greeks were trying to get everyone to follow their religion (paganism) and any Jew who remained faithful to his or her Jewish faith was put to death. This was the first time in the history of the world that people were persecuted for their beliefs. The book of Daniel tried to offer the Jewish people hope: hope of a savior. This salvation comes from one like a "son of man" whom God endows with kingship and power. Our reading is one of Daniel's visions and it first describes God who is called the Ancient One - indicating God's eternity. The term "son of man" means simply a human being, but this "son of man" would be unique and would be the savior of God's people. This was the favorite title Jesus used in referring to himself. The glory of God is described in today's first reading. It is shown through Christ in his Transfiguration, which is described in today's gospel (Mk. 9, 2-10), and in today's second reading from the Second Letter of St. Peter (1, 16-19).

HOMILY – Last Sunday I said that for the next four weeks we would be hearing from the sixth chapter of St. John on the Eucharist. I hadn't looked ahead to see that this Sunday fell on August 6th which is the feast of the

Transfiguration. Although we hear about the Transfiguration every year on the second Sunday of Lent, the actual feast of the Transfiguration is on August 6. It is an important enough feast that it replaces the normal Sunday liturgy.

Tradition identifies Mt. Tabor as the mountain of the Transfiguration. It's quite a climb to get to the top. There is a chapel on top of the mountain commemorating the occasion of the Transfiguration. I said Mass there sixteen years ago when I went with a study group to the Holy Land. They had cars and buses to take us up the mountain. I'm not surprised that Peter, James and John fell asleep, as St. Luke tells us in his gospel, when they went there with Jesus. They didn't have cars and buses and they would have been very tired when they got to the top. But when they woke up their efforts to make it up to the top of that mountain with Jesus were well rewarded. "It is good that we are here," Peter said. "Let us make three tents here: one for you, one for Moses and one for Elijah." It sounds to me as if they were ready to stay there for several weeks, it was such an awesome experience. As wonderful as it was, Jesus' work wasn't finished and neither was theirs. They had to come back down to earth.

Most of us, I'm sure, have had moments when we've felt God's presence and closeness and special love, or when we knew God was helping us with some problem. But I'm sure there are few, if any of us, who have experienced anything like the Transfiguration. We may be a mystic and have ecstatic experiences in prayer or we may be a saint who receives visions of Jesus or Mary. Other than that, we've probably not experienced anything like the Transfiguration and may find it difficult to relate to. But we can learn from it.

(1) We can learn that God has great glory reserved for us until, as the second reading tells us, "day dawns and the morning star rises in your hearts."

(2) We can learn from what God spoke on the holy mountain about Jesus: "this is my beloved Son, listen to him." This is not something new, of course, but it doesn't hurt to be reminded once again that we must listen to him.

(3) We can learn that we cannot expect mountaintop experiences every day when we pray, when we receive the sacraments, when we keep the Commandments. There are those moments when we get a lot of consolation and good feelings from our faith and our prayers. Then there are those moments when prayer is dry, when our faith is exactly what that word means, believing only on the word of another and not feeling anything except that we're in a desert. The apostles were with Jesus three years and there was only one experience like the Transfiguration, and only three of them experienced it. Our religion can't be based on feelings. It's based on faith in God and love for God and for one another. Sometimes we feel it and sometimes we don't. It's not how we feel it that counts, but how we live it.

(4) Another thing we can learn from the Transfiguration is that we can't always trust appearances. In appearance Jesus looked pretty much like the rest of us. Artists have pictured him with a halo, but I'm sure there was no halo when people saw him every day. The gospels would have remarked about it if there were. For a brief moment on Mt. Tabor, the apostles saw and heard things that indicated there was a lot more to Jesus than they ever imagined.

Today, as we come to Mass, our faith calls us to look

beyond appearances. When we receive Communion, we receive what appears to be a wafer of bread and a sip of wine, but faith in the power and the words of Jesus tells us this host and cup offers us so much more. It is food for eternal life. We pray as always that the Lord will help us to know his presence with us today, and if we do not experience that presence, we pray for the faith to be able to see beyond appearances and still be able to say as Peter did on the mountain: "it is good that we are here."

18th Sunday in Ordinary Time
August, 2006

INTRODUCTION – (Exodus 16: 2-4. 12-15 Ephesians 4: 17. 20-24; John 6: 24-35) Last Sunday we heard about Jesus feeding a multitude of people (over 5000 men the gospel tells us) with five loaves of bread and two fish. It must have been a powerful experience as it is the only miracle recorded in all four gospels other than the miracle of Christ's resurrection. St. John gives us further indication of the magnitude of this miracle in that he tells us there were twelve baskets of left overs from the five loaves of bread and two fish. It was impressive enough that the people wanted to make Jesus their king. But Jesus did not want to be the kind of king they had in mind. So he sent his apostles off in a boat and he went into the hills to be by himself and pray. Later on that evening he joined his apostles which is a story all its own, for they were still in the boat and Jesus came to them walking on the water. Today's gospel begins when the crowd meet up with Jesus later on at Capernaum.

The first reading gives us some historical background for the gospel. It tells how God fed his people with manna 1300 years earlier on their way from Egypt to the promised land. In the conversation the people are having with Jesus in the gospel they refer to the event of God feeding his people with manna in the desert.

HOMILY – The clock in a restaurant window had stopped at a few minutes past noon. One day a patron asked the owner, "Do you know that the clock in your window has stopped?" The owner answered, "It hasn't been working for months. But you would be surprised to know how many people look at that clock, think they are hungry, and come in to get something to eat."

There's more to life than satisfying our physical hunger. That's what Jesus is trying to tell people in today's gospel. He said, "You are not looking for me because you have seen signs but because you have eaten your fill of the loaves." A sign always points to something else. An exit sign tells us how to leave a building or a parking lot. Smoke tells us there is fire somewhere. A no smoking sign tells us not to smoke. Jesus wanted to tell people that the miracle of the loaves pointed to something more. But they didn't see that. They didn't know it was a sign. They were content with having their stomachs filled. That's why he said, "You are not looking for me because you have seen signs but because you have eaten your fill of the loaves." They wanted only what they wanted, not what he wanted to give them. In our relationship with God, we must ask ourselves, are we interested only in getting God to give us what we want, or are we willing to work so that God can give us what God wants for us?

Notice how this word 'work' sneaks in here. (It's one of those nasty four letter words most of us don't like to hear.) Jesus said, "Do not work for food that perishes but for the food that endures for eternal life, which the Son of Man will give you." The people ask (and this is a literal translation of the Greek text), "What can we do to work the works of God?" Jesus said, "This is the work of God, that you believe in the one he sent." Faith takes work. It is not a cakewalk. It is not for the faint hearted. Keeping the commandments, praying when it feels like no one is listening, going to Mass when we would rather stay in bed, believing in what we cannot see, loving people who are not very lovable, forgiving those who hurt us, trusting that God really loves us when we feel the world is down on us, keeping our faith in the face of scandals in the Church. These are some of the things that take real work. We cannot accomplish anything really worthwhile in life without work – and that's true of our faith too. We'll get out of our faith what we put into it. The current attitude among many is that God is good and we're all going to heaven in the end, no matter what, so why sweat it? Well, God is good, and he tried to guide us in the right direction and he even died on the cross to help us get there, but God cannot save us if we are too lazy or too busy or too indifferent to do our part.

There's one other line in today's gospel I want to call attention to. Jesus said "Whoever comes to me will never hunger…" It hurts to be hungry. We have all felt it at times – not as bad as some people in other parts of the world – but we know what it feels like nonetheless. If we didn't feel that pain from time to time we would probably all starve to death. There was a good article in *Reader's Digest* last month entitled "Hungry all the time. How to turn off the switch." The point of the article was that there are certain foods we eat that significantly increase the feeling of hunger in us, and that cause us to overeat. By avoiding certain foods we will be less hungry. You can probably guess what those foods are. They're things like white bread, white rice, bagels, donuts, soft drinks, ice cream, sweet cereals, French fries, etc. Our society offers us lots of spiritual junk food too. It nourishes us momentarily but still leaves our inner person feeling empty and hungry for something more. Jesus promises to fill our inner selves so that we can know true fulfillment and peace when he tells us "Whoever comes to me will never hunger..." And that's what brought us here today. He is the true bread that gives life to the world. Amen.

19th Sunday in Ordinary Time
August 13, 2006

INTRODUCTION – (1 Kings 19, 4-8; Ephesians 4, 30 – 5, 2; John 6, 41-51) Eight hundred fifty years before Christ there lived in Israel a queen with an evil reputation named Jezebel. Among her many goals in life was to eliminate the Israelite religion. There lived also in Israel at this time the prophet Elijah whose life was dedicated to serving the one true God, Yahweh. Naturally these two would clash. In a very dramatic and powerful confrontation on Mt. Carmel, a place now known as Haifa, the prophet Elijah worked a miracle that demonstrated that Yahweh was truly God, while the gods of Jezebel were nothing at all. Jezebel was not a happy loser in this confrontation, and she sent her army after Elijah in order to kill him. Elijah took off running. Today's first reading finds him in the southern part of the Holy Land, hungry, tired and depressed. But God took care of him and gave him special food that strengthened him to be able to walk for 40 days through desert wildness to Mt. Horeb, the mountain in the Sinai Peninsula where God gave Moses the 10 Commandments.

This passage has been chosen because of the special food God gave Elijah. The passage connects with the gospel where Jesus tells us he is the bread that will strengthen us on our journey through life and into eternal life.

HOMILY – Our readings today are about food, something that is near and dear to all of us. It's near and dear to all of us not only because it's something we enjoy, but something we need to have in order to live.

Two weeks ago the gospel was about Jesus feeding a great crowd - over 5000 people with five barley loaves and a couple of dried fish. After he fed them, they wanted to make him their king and why wouldn't they? But Jesus came to give us something more than free food. And so he got away from this crowd that were intent on making him a king until they settled down. When they found him again, he told them you're looking for me not because you've seen signs (indicating they couldn't see more deeply into what Jesus did), but you're looking for me simply because you've had your stomach filled. He came, he told them, in order to give them food that would bring them eternal life. Of course they wanted that too. So he told them that food was himself: "I am the bread of life… I am the living bread that came down from heaven; whoever eats this bread will live forever." That was not easy for them to swallow (if you'll pardon the expression). In spite of the great miracle he had worked, they failed to believe in him. But he did not back down.

If you read through this section of St. John you will see there are two different ways to understand this expression that Jesus is the bread of life. We Catholics almost automatically presume that the idea that Jesus is the bread of life means the Eucharist, and it does, but it means something that precedes the Eucharist. The first way to understand this idea is to understand that Jesus feeds us through his word and our acceptance of that word. In other words, Jesus is the bread of life because we believe what he teaches us. This is one big reason such a large part of the Mass is dedicated to hearing God's word. It is through hearing and believing that we are fed: our mind is fed, our spirit is fed, our heart is fed. God's word influences our thoughts, our attitudes, our actions, the way we treat others, our attitude toward God and toward ourselves. This openness of our mind and heart to his word is a source of eternal life for us.

As we read on through this chapter, the idea that Jesus is the bread of life in the Eucharist begins to be developed. It will be developed in the next couple of weeks, but it is introduced here with the words: "the bread that I will give is my flesh." I would like to digress here for a moment. St. John devotes a lot of his gospel to the Last Supper, but he does not tell us about the institution of the Eucharist. It is in this place that he does. Notice the words "the bread that I will give is my flesh..." Notice how closely the words parallel what we hear at the consecration: "this (the bread) is my body." The *bread* that I will give *is my flesh*." As I said, we will hear Jesus say this more emphatically in the next couple of weeks, so emphatically and clearly in fact that those who had been ready to make him a king said he was crazy and they walked away.

Modern science has discovered many things about food. It has told us about foods that are healthy and foods that are unhealthy, foods that can help heal us and foods that contribute to sickness, foods that can even affect our moods and our energy. We've learned from science about vitamins and minerals, but we know we can't just stop eating and just take one big vitamin pill. Scientists tell us there are still elements hidden in food that affect our health and well-being positively or negatively that they haven't discovered yet. Although we've all seen vitamin pills, vitamins themselves are tiny molecules that we can't see with the unaided eye. We just have to take it on faith that they're in the vitamin pills we take or the food that nutritionists tell us is healthy food.

We have to take it on faith, too, that there is a lot in Jesus' teaching and his sacraments that we cannot see and will never see in this world with our eyes. We can only believe what our ears tell us. When we look at the host we see what looks like bread. What we hear, though, are the words of Jesus, "The bread that I will give is my flesh." Jesus is the bread of life. Believing in him, living according to his word and receiving his sacraments are life-giving. He gives us a life that is abundant, a life that is eternal, a life that will bring greater joy that we can now imagine. We thank the Lord for this gift of divine nourishment he gives us today.

Vigil of the Feast of the Assumption
August 14, 2006

INTRODUCTION AT THE VIGIL – It is a dogma of our faith that at the end of her life, Mary, like her son, was taken body and soul into heavenly glory. This is the meaning of the Assumption, whose vigil we celebrate this evening.

Our first reading (I Chronicles 15, 3-4,15-16; 16, 1-2) is about the Ark of the Covenant, the sacred gold plated box that contained the Ten Commandments. On the top of the Ark there were two golden angels and the Israelites envisioned God's throne positioned above the angels. The Ark was the unique symbol of God's presence with Israel. It was constructed in the desert after Moses and the Israelites left Egypt. It led them into the Promised Land. Often it was taken into battle with them. When King David established his capital in Jerusalem about the year 1000 BC, he brought the Ark there. Today's reading describes this solemn and joyful occasion. After the temple was built, the Ark was placed in the Holy of Holies and there it remained for 400 years until the Babylonians destroyed the temple and walked off with the Ark.

There was a very imaginative Indiana Jones movie that was built on the theme of finding the lost Ark. It's anyone's guess whether it was destroyed or lies buried with some past civilization.

In Christian symbolism, Mary is sometimes referred to as the Ark of the Covenant. Just as God was present in a special way wherever the Ark was taken, so God was present with Mary in a most special way when she carried within her womb the only Son of God, Jesus our Savior.

The early Christians also saw Jerusalem as a symbol of heaven. With all the turmoil in the Holy Land, it's not a very fitting symbol in recent years, but that symbolism is reflected in today's first reading. The Ark being taken up to Jerusalem symbolizes Mary being taken body and soul into the heavenly kingdom.

HOMILY – A woman exclaimed how fortunate Jesus' mother was to have had such a son. (Lk. 11, 27-28) On first hearing this it sounds as if Jesus is denying anything special about Mary. Would Jesus put down the loving mother who bore him and raised him? Certainly not! However, Jesus was saying there was something even more important about Mary than all that. Most important of all was her willingness to do all that God asked of her. That made her more one with her Son than anything else. When God's angel asked her if she would be the mother of our Savior, her answer was: "Let it be done to me as you say." Surely her faith was tested many times, but she never wavered in her faith or in her obedience to God's will. She was the perfect and number one disciple of Jesus in always being willing to do what God asked of her. She remained faithful even during her most bitter trial, watching her son Jesus die on a cross. Jesus' response to the woman in today's gospel identifies what it is that truly makes Mary great.

In our society those who are related to important people make a big deal of that relationship. With God it's not that way. It's our relationship with Jesus in a spiritual way that matters. And Mary was absolutely the best in this regard. Christ came, as he says in St. John's gospel, that we might have the fullness of life. Our faith in the resurrection tells us our bodies too will share in that fullness. But it was only fitting that Mary should be first in line to share in the fullness of salvation that Jesus came to bring us.

Today's feast is a feast to honor Mary and it is fitting that we do so, since God himself has so honored her. But it is also a feast that shows us God's plans for all those who faithfully follow God's will.

Feast of the Assumption
August 15, 2006

INTRODUCTION ON THE FEAST – (Rev. 11, 19a; 12, 1-6a, 10ab; I Cor. 15, 20-27; Lk. 1, 39-56) The book of Revelation is highly symbolic. Some of the symbolism is quite obvious while it requires a fairly extensive knowledge of Scripture to interpret some of the other symbols. In today's first reading we hear about a woman, a child and a dragon. The dragon is the devil and the powers of evil at work in the world. The child is Christ. The woman in our reading has a double symbolism. She stands for Mary, the physical mother of Jesus Christ, and she stands for the Church, our spiritual mother who brings Jesus Christ to birth in us through faith and the sacraments. In today's passage the woman is rescued from the powers of the dragon and is described in great glory. This too has a double symbolism. It symbolizes the glory of Mary in the assumption. It also symbolizes God's faithful people whom he will rescue from evil and will bring, in the resurrection from the dead, into the glory of heaven.

HOMILY – It is recorded nowhere in Scripture when, where or how Mary died. Nor do the Scriptures tell us about her assumption. It has been a part, however, of the very ancient tradition of the Church that Mary was assumed bodily into heavenly glory when her life here on earth was ended. One early document referring to this event comes from the Bishop of Jerusalem in 451, St. Juvenal. He was asked by the emperor of Constantinople to bring the body of Mary to Constantinople. He replied to the emperor that Mary had died in the presence of all the apostles. But her tomb, when opened upon the request of St. Thomas, was found empty. Thus the apostles concluded that her body was taken up to heaven as Jesus was.

Some people belittle tradition as if it were unimportant. They claim to believe only the Scriptures. Yet, if we stop and think about it, we would have no Scriptures without tradition for the Scriptures came from the Church's tradition. Many of the letters of Paul were written before the gospels and there probably was a written list of many of Jesus' sayings that no longer exists. But of our four gospels, Mark's is the first that was written, and it was written about 40 years after Jesus' ascension. I say all of this so you can see the importance of tradition. So to say that the knowledge of the Assumption of Mary came from the very early tradition of the Church is to give a lot of weight to this teaching. But to eliminate any doubt as to whether Mary actually was assumed into heavenly glory, the Holy Father, Pope Pius XII, after reviewing the belief of the Church through the ages, made it a dogma of our faith in 1950.

In today's gospel Mary is a young girl going to visit her much older cousin Elizabeth. Mary had just been visited by the angel, and she had accepted the invitation to be the mother of the Savior God was sending to his people. So she is at this moment pregnant and not married. And she is not pregnant by her spouse to be, Joseph. It was not a happy situation for a girl in that society. She could have been rejected by her husband to be, she could have been rejected by her family or could even have been put to death. Yet she is full of trust in God and praises God's greatness and God's goodness. There is no expression of "poor me." She is entirely focused on God. Mary shows us how to be trusting and in her assumption she shows us where that trust will lead us.

Today's feast honors Mary, for God himself has honored her. In her openness to God and in her willingness to always do whatever God wanted, God rewarded her in a unique way. But today's feast also is a source of hope for us. Christ came, as he says in St. John's gospel, that we might have the fullness of life. Our faith tells us our bodies too will share in that fullness. So Mary is allowed to enjoy ahead of time what

God's plan is for all of us who are faithful in following him and serving him.

20th Sunday in Ordinary Time
August 20, 2006

INTRODUCTION – (Proverbs 9, 1-6; Ephesians 5, 15-20; John 6, 51-58) The ninth chapter of the book of Proverbs speaks symbolically of two women: one is named Lady Wisdom and the other is Dame Folly. Both are like hotel owners who invite people to their hotels. Lady Wisdom offers an elegant and lavish banquet for her guests. Those who share her hospitality are rewarded with joy and an abundance of life. Those who accept the invitation of Dame Folly are walking into a trap that will result in their death. The first reading today describes only the invitation of Lady Wisdom. The columns that are part of her house symbolize stability, while the number seven symbolizes perfection.

It is rare that the second reading corresponds with the first reading, but today it does, as St. Paul encourages us not to be foolish but to be wise with a wisdom only God's Holy Spirit can give us.

HOMILY – Some time ago I read about a mother who had a frightening experience with her two year old son. She found him playing with an empty bottle of heart medicine. She was unable to get him to tell her what happened to the pills that were in the bottle, so she spent six tortured hours with him in the hospital as the staff tired to pump his stomach. Fortunately he hadn't swallowed any of the pills, but if he had they could have killed him. Now this mother spends most of her free time speaking to parent groups warning them how easily children can swallow the wrong stuff. Statistics show that more than a million children under six are victims of accidental poisoning in a year's time. How does a child tell the difference between Sweet-Tarts and Tums, Tic Tacs and Motrin, Hershey's chocolate and Ex-Lax, Pine-Sol and apple juice. If you are a child and can't read labels, how can you tell which is which?

It's not just children that can be fooled by look-alikes. How often have we bought fruit flavored drinks in the supermarket that have never seen a piece of fruit? They just look and taste like they have. A better example is the famous placebo. When doctors or pharmaceutical companies test medicine, they also create a pill or liquid that looks exactly like the real medicine but contains no medicine at all. By giving the real medicine and the placebo to two separate groups they can see whether the medicine they are testing is of any value.

Most of you can probably see where this is headed. You can't always judge something by appearances. This is what Jesus is talking about today. We cannot tell the difference between consecrated and unconsecrated hosts or consecrated or unconsecrated wine by looking at it or smelling it or tasting it or even putting it in a test tube. We can only take it on faith the bread and wine that has been consecrated at Mass is Jesus' body and blood and that it is food that will give us eternal life. He tells us: "The bread that I will give is my flesh for the life of the world." In case the point isn't clear, he says it with emphasis: "Amen, amen, I say to you, unless you eat the flesh of the Son of Man and drink his blood, you do not have life within you." Amen, amen means 'I am not kidding. I am not fooling around. This is for real, this is serious.' The only way we know this is so is because Jesus told us so. Just as a parent has to tell his or her child "This is good for you," or "this is not good for you," so also God tells us what is truly for our good and what isn't. He is telling us today, the Eucharist is truly good for us. We have to decide whether to believe our eyes, which tell us one thing, or our ears, which hear the words of Jesus, that the consecrated bread and wine are infinitely more than what they appear to be.

Hopefully, we are saying to ourselves, "If Jesus said it, it has to be true and I believe it." But saying we believe it and doing something about it are two different things. If we really believe something we act on it. If I told you I was going to hand out hundred dollar bills tomorrow afternoon at 2:00, if you really believed me you probably would show up, unless you felt sorry for me and didn't want to take my money. If your favorite program on the radio or TV was suddenly interrupted by an emergency announcement that said there was a missile headed right in our direction and we believed it, we would probably run for cover, unless we have a death wish. If my doctor tells me to do something and I believe what he says, I will do it, unless I enjoy pain or I just want to die early. In other words, faith is not just in our head, it is also in the way we live. Are we interested in deepening our relationship with God? If we believe the Eucharist is Christ, that this sacred food gives us eternal life, then isn't making time to come to Mass whenever we can and receiving the Eucharist whenever possible something we would want to do?

Our first two readings encourage us to be wise people. A foolish person is limited mentally; they see things superficially. A wise person sees beyond the obvious. If we adopt the vision that God gives us, a vision that goes beyond what we can figure out for ourselves, a vision we call faith, we are the wisest people of all.

21st Sunday in Ordinary Time
August 27, 2006

INTRODUCTION − (Jos 24, 1-2a. 15-17. 18b; Ephesians 5, 21-32; John 6, 60-69) Shortly after God's people arrived in the Promised Land, Joshua, who became their leader after Moses died, gathered the people together to renew their covenant with Yahweh. They enthusiastically chose to commit themselves to follow God faithfully. Unfortunately, as we know, their descendants were seduced by the pagan practices of the Canaanites who previously inhabited the Land. This first reading prepares us for the gospel where many of Jesus' disciples, unlike the followers of Moses and Joshua, made the choice not to stay with Jesus because they couldn't accept his teaching on the Eucharist.

Often when men hear today's second reading, they only hear part of it. They hear the part where St. Paul says "wives should be subordinate to their husbands," but miss the first sentence which says "Be subordinate to one another out of reverence for Christ." In other words, married love involves commitment and mutuality. In the end, it should resemble the love between Christ and the Church.

HOMILY − Today's gospel describes what must have been a very sad day for Jesus. John tells us most of Jesus' followers walked away from him. The day before, they were ready to make him a king; for he had fed them (a great crowd) miraculously with five loaves of bread and two fish. When he told them he was going to give them his flesh to eat and his blood to drink, they thought he was crazy. As Jesus saw them leaving he asked his apostles if they wanted to leave too. What Jesus had been saying was so serious and so important that he was willing to let everyone walk away from him if they chose.

There was no way to compromise on what he said, no way to water it down. The real bread he came to offer them was himself, he told them, and it was food that would give them eternal life. When they questioned this, he only said it more emphatically and more clearly. Their response was: "This saying is hard; who can accept it?" What was hard was their own minds. They wouldn't open their minds to something they couldn't understand. In all of this we get an ideal picture of what we call "faith." Faith is accepting what we cannot understand, what we cannot prove, what we cannot figure out. We just accept something as true because we trust Jesus who tells us it is so.

Notice, Jesus didn't call the people back who were walking away from him. He didn't say, "Wait people, I'm just talking figuratively. I'm just talking symbolically. I don't mean you really have to eat my flesh and drink my blood! You misunderstand me." He knew there was no misunderstanding; they understood him perfectly and he let them go.

If you want proof from the bible for the real presence of Christ in the Eucharist, you'll find lots of proof, but I think this is the clearest proof you'll find. We might hear the words of Jesus at the last supper: "This is my body" and quibble over the definition of "is," but there can be little doubt that Jesus is telling us in this event that the Eucharist is really his body and blood. Those who cannot understand how it can be try to tell us the Eucharist is only a reminder of Jesus' death for us, or it's only a symbol, or some how Jesus comes to us along with the bread and wine but it's not really changed. They are in effect saying Jesus didn't really mean what he said.

We who believe in the Eucharist as the body and blood of Christ do not understand how it could be any better than any one else. And theologians and philosophers have given it their best effort but we still don't know "how" it can be. So it still comes down to faith. The apostles stayed with Jesus, not because they understood any better than the crowd, but because they trusted Jesus: "You have the words of eternal life. We have come to believe and are convinced that you are the Holy One of God."

Let me add just one quick thought. Although we seldom think of it, we eat flesh all the time. We eat the flesh of chickens, fish, pigs, cows, lambs. That's what keeps us alive. We can't see it but we know there is energy hidden in all this food and it sustains our life. The flesh of Jesus that we receive is not dead flesh (like the flesh of a chicken or a cow), but it is his living and risen body and blood. In Jesus' flesh is hidden energy, divine energy that will nourish us with eternal life. And the only way to approach it so that it is life giving is to approach the Eucharist with faith and trust and love.

22nd Sunday in Ordinary Time
September 3, 2006

INTRODUCTION – (Dt. 4, 1-2. 6-8; James 1, 17-18. 21b-22. 27; Mark 7, 1-8. 14-15. 21-23) Today's first reading takes us back about 13 centuries before Christ. God's people, after their escape from Egypt and their 40 year sojourn in the desert, are getting close to crossing the Jordan and entering the Promised Land. Moses was still with them and he knew he would die before they crossed the Jordan. So he had some last words instructing and encouraging God's people before his departure. In essence he is telling God's people that God loves his people and he wants them to prosper. They will do so only if they keep God's laws.

HOMILY – There is nothing subtle about today's readings. They are straightforward and blunt. In today's gospel, the religious leaders of Jesus' day were accusing him of ignoring their laws and traditions. Jesus turned the tables on them and told them they're missing the main point of what religion is all about. Besides contradicting some of God's laws, Jesus condemned them because they stressed only external observance. Jesus reminds them (and us) that true religion is about a change of heart.

In our society we encounter an overwhelming amount of laws, some from God, some from our religious leaders and many from government and civil authority. Law is important. Without law, civilization cannot survive. Without law there is chaos and anarchy. At the same time freedom is important. We live in a society where too many people think freedom means doing whatever they want without having to answer to any authority. Without law there would be no freedom for we would be spending all our energy simply trying to avoid being annihilated. Moses reminded God's people in today's first reading that if they kept God's laws they would be admired by their contemporaries and they would prosper. We have to balance the restrictions that laws place upon us with the freedom we want to enjoy. This requires maturity to be able to keep that balance and most of us manage to do a fairly good job of that.

Sometimes when we get tempted we might think: swell if no one is watching and I don't get caught, maybe I can get by with doing something I shouldn't be doing or avoiding something I should. When we think that way, we're becoming like the Pharisees and thinking only about the externals.

Now, external observance is very important. We

might feel like hitting someone over the head with a club, but it is a better thing not to do it. St. James tells us today "Be doers of the word and not hearers only." God's ten commandments are mostly about external behavior: worship God, respect his name, honor our parents, do not kill, lie, steal, commit adultery. Only the last two are about what goes on in our hearts: when we want to take possession of what belongs to someone else. Our feelings are not always the purest or the best, but if we behave in a kindly and appropriate manner, that is good. And it is often through doing the right thing that our hearts are changed. For example, I may not always feel like praying, but by trying to pray anyway, I am more likely to develop an interior spirit of prayer. Of course, Jesus wants us to do what is right, but he wants more. He wants nothing less than for our hearts to be filled with his love and grace.

Whether someone is watching or not, it's when we have a right heart that we do the right thing,. That's a high level of moral maturity. It's a goal we try to teach our children, it's a goal we strive for ourselves. Until we get to that point, we stumble along with prayer and the sacraments to help us on the way.

23rd Sunday in Ordinary Time
September 10, 2006

INTRODUCTION – (Isaiah 35, 4-7a; James 2, 1-5; Mark 7, 31-37) The prophet Isaiah is speaking to God's people during their captivity in Babylon: "Be strong, fear not! Here is your God...he comes to save you." God's salvation is expressed in terms of healing the blind and the deaf, the lame and the mute. The desert would come alive with rivers and springs and an abundance of life giving water. The reading prepares us for the gospel where Jesus heals a man who was a deaf mute. Jesus' healing work was a work of compassion, but it also announced in a dramatic way God's saving presence among his people. In our own times of trial we need to hear these words of Isaiah again and again: "Here is your God...he comes to save you." The second reading today, from St. James, warns us against judging other people by their material success or lack of it.

HOMILY – It wasn't bad enough that the man in today's gospel lacked the ability to hear the beautiful sounds of nature or to engage in meaningful conversation with family or friends. Education was out of the question. Employment opportunities would have been limited or non-existent. And on top of all that, any sickness or disability in that culture was seen as a punishment for sin. So society would have seen him as an evil individual, cursed by God... not a happy existence. Jesus was asked to help him, and he did.

Let me point out two important features of today's gospel:

1.) Other people brought the man who needed healing to Jesus. We need the help of others to find the Lord: a parish community that is spiritual, friends who are spiritual and who can influence our faith in a positive way, books that can teach us. Sometimes God uses us to be that other person that someone needs to bring them to God.

2.) Jesus took the man off by himself – away from the crowd. It sounds like a contradiction of my first point, but it's not. Even though others may help us find our way to Christ, if we are going to grow in his grace and love, we also need to spend time alone with him. If we always have to be entertained, to have TV or radio or be absorbed in doing something... if we do not make time for quiet time in our life so we can hear our Lord speak to us, it's not likely we will hear him very well...if at all.

We tend to take so many of our gifts for granted, including the gift of being able to hear. What joy must have come to this man whom Jesus healed, and what joy must Jesus have felt to have been able to help him.

Yet even for those of us who can hear, how much deafness there is! I'm not talking about physical deafness but about one person not hearing what the other is saying. We see it for example between spouses and between parents and children. This deafness brings such pain at times. This is one of the most important ingredients in marriage: communication; really hearing one another. St. James in today's second reading talks about people who have no social standing – how often we are deaf to their needs. We need healing in many areas.

Another kind of deafness for which we need healing is deafness to God's word. How often do we hear the Scriptures on Sunday and we feel as if they had nothing to say to us? It's not that the Scriptures have nothing to say, and it's not that some are more difficult to interpret than others, but if we never hear God speaking to us through them, we need to ask for the ability to hear what he is telling us. Once I was counseling a man who was feeling very anxious and I just happened to open the Bible to the section of Isaiah which we just heard in today's first reading. I read: "Say to those whose hearts are frightened: be strong, fear not! Here is your God, he has come to save you!" I am sure it was what God wanted him to hear and I know he heard the words with his ears, but not with his heart. His fears were speaking to him louder that the words from Isaiah and God's word gave him no peace. He needed Jesus to touch the ears of his heart to hear the word God wanted him to hear.

Hearing another, including God, is a skill that takes practice and it is also a gift that God can help us with if we ask him. In our time of reflection, let us take a moment of silence to thank God for the gift of hearing, and let us pray for healing in those areas of our lives where we are unable to hear, or do not want to hear.

24th Sunday in Ordinary Time
September 17, 2006

INTRODUCTION – (Isaiah 50, 5-9a; James 2, 14-18; Mark 8, 27-35) The book of the prophet Isaiah contains four poems commonly referred to as Servant Songs. They are mysterious passages, because no one is sure whom they were originally meant to refer to: the prophet Isaiah, some other specific individual, or Israel as a whole. They describe one whom God had chosen from before birth not only to serve him and to serve God's people, but to be a light to the nations and to bring God's salvation to the ends of the earth. It's amazing how perfectly these Servant Songs, written over 500 years before Christ, describe Jesus. Today's passage describes how God's Servant would run into a lot of resistance and even persecution, but God would stand by him during all his trials.

HOMILY – Caesarea Philippi is located in the northern part of Galilee, near the headwaters of the Jordan. Unlike most of the holy land which is fairly dry, Caesarea Philippi is in an area where there is lot of water and vegetation. At the time of Jesus there was a shrine dedicated to the Greek god Pan. Pan was that Greek god whose head and torso was human, but the lower part of his body was the body of a goat. Pan was the god of nature, woods and fields, flocks and shepherds. He loved to romp through the fields playing his flute leading a group of dancing nymphs. He was blamed for striking terror in people who had to travel through fields and forests at night, and this is where we get the word "panic." This is probably more than you wanted to know about Greek mythology, but in the cliffs around Caesarea Philippi there are carved a number of niches where statues of Greek gods and goddesses were enshrined. Surrounded by all these gods and goddesses, Jesus asked his disciples: "Who do people say *I* am?" Then he asked: "Who do *you* say *I* am?" Here is the true God, the Lord of all creation, asking "Am I on a level with all of those other gods and goddesses? Do you think I am something greater or something less?" Peter said "You are the Christ, i.e., you are the Messiah, the long awaited savior." But he still had much to learn. They originally believed Jesus came to save only the chosen people. And they didn't believe he would do it by suffering. Jesus knew his scriptures and he had insights that penetrated life's mysteries far beyond the capability of any other human being. He knew that by being faithful to his mission of speaking truth he would pay for it by shedding his blood. But he knew also as God's faithful servant, God would stand by him, he would not be disgraced, he would not be put to shame.

Jesus question "Who do you say that I am?" continues to echo down through the centuries. Much of history has been shaped by the way various people have answered this question. It's a question that each of us must ask of ourselves.

It's a question that is the subject of a recent publication of the Congregation for the Doctrine of the Faith. The document entitled *Dominus Jesus* stresses that Jesus Christ is the only savior. It does not say that others who do not know Christ cannot be saved. It simply says that those who are saved are saved by grace that comes from Jesus Christ. He is the only savior, the only Son of God, the one who came to show us the way to God. And what is the way to God? This is where the document continues on.

I think, the headlines for the *Catholic Telegraph* this week were misleading at best and inflammatory at worst. They stated "Catholicism is necessary for salvation." It sounds as if they are saying you have to be a Catholic or you won't be saved. I have to admit, I haven't read the document *Dominus Jesus*, but from what I could get out of the article about the document, it's not saying that at all. What I understood is that it's saying all churches are not the same. In other words the document is trying to combat what it sees to be a popular attitude that "one religion is as good as another." I agree that all religions are not created equal. If one religion were as good as another, I would go looking for one that would be a bit more convenient for me, (maybe a little easier) – or I could even start my own and run it the way I think it ought to be run. That's what a lot of other people have done. But I am convinced that the Catholic Church is most true to the way Christ founded his Church to be. However, there is a flavor of triumphalism in the article, and perhaps in the document itself that reminds me of the days when Catholics thought no one was going to get to heaven except them. It's kind of like what the apostles thought about Jesus' mission. He was there only to save the Jews. Jesus sure surprised them. And I think a lot of us are going to be surprised when we get to heaven as to whom we see, or whom we don't see there. I believe the Catholic Church is the Church Christ established. The gospels make it clear that Jesus gave his Church a visible structure under the authority of the apostles and St. Peter. They are succeeded by the bishops and the Holy Father today. When I think about all of this I like to use the image of TV reception. When TV first came out, the reception was not very great. Some channels come in clearer than others. I think that is like the various churches trying to bring us a picture of God and his teachings. Some do a better job than others. I think the Catholic Church does the best job, but I'll be the first one to say the Catholic Church is not perfect either. I love to quote the statement of Fr. Andrew Greeley who said, "if you ever find a perfect church, by all means, join it. But just be sure to know that once *you* join it, it will no longer be perfect!"

The document itself is talking about churches, not about individual church members. Just because I am a Catholic, I cannot claim to be better or holier than my Protestant, or Jewish or Buddhist neighbor. Even though I believe that the Catholic Church is the best of all churches, that it gives me the clearest picture of who God is and what God wants of me, that doesn't mean I am a better person than someone who is not Catholic. I might be in worse trouble at the Last Judgment because I didn't use the opportunities and graces that were available to me. St. James reminds us today: "Faith of itself, if it does not have works, is dead." One mother recently told me about her child who was raised Catholic but was attending a Protestant church. I know it will shock some people to know that I told the mother, "I'm glad at least he's going to church. That's better than a lot of people who call themselves Catholics but seldom show up at Church." If a person doesn't live like they are supposed to, it doesn't matter what they call themselves: Catholic, Protestant, Jewish, Hindu or whatever; it means nothing.

All this talk about which Church is better, which Church is truer to the Church Christ founded, must not cause us to forget about the great importance of unity for Christ's followers. This is something that Christ fervently desired and prayed for for his Church and it is something we should not cease to pray for or work for.

25th Sunday in Ordinary Time
September 24, 2006

INTRODUCTION – (Wisdom 2, 12. 17-20; James 3, 16 – 4, 3; Mark 9, 30-37) Thanks to Alexander the Great who, in his day, conquered everything between Egypt and India, the Greeks ruled all of the Middle East and they controlled it for a little more than 250 years. This area included the Holy Land. During that period of time, the Greek rulers decided all nations should accept Greek culture and religion. The Jews were forced to give up their belief in the one God they had worshipped since the days of Abraham and Moses. Those who did not submit were persecuted or killed. Today's reading from the book of Wisdom describes what the Jews who converted to paganism thought of those who where faithful to Yahweh. The faithful Jew is sarcastically called "the just one" and his or her belief in God is ridiculed. The first reading connects with the gospel in that Jesus who is truly the "just one" predicts the suffering he will have to face for remaining faithful to God's work.

HOMILY – A young couple invited their elderly pastor to dinner on Sunday. While they were in the kitchen getting the dinner ready, the minister asked their young son what they were having for dinner. "Goat," the little boy replied. "Goat?" the surprised pastor asked. "Are you sure?" "Yep," said the little boy. "I heard Dad say to Mom this morning: 'Today is just as good a day as any to have the old goat for dinner.'"

Children have a way of bringing us down to earth. Jesus used a child to bring his disciples back down to earth. Even after he tells them what terrible things he would have to go through, his disciples were busy arguing over which of them was the greatest. You can imagine that in their minds they were already picturing themselves sitting in a position of prestige and importance next to their Messiah after he drove the Romans out of their land as they expected that he would do. Then Jesus bursts their bubble. "If anyone wishes to be first, he shall be last of all and the servant of all."

Notice Jesus didn't condemn the apostles for wanting to be great. As a matter of fact he taught them how to be great and how to be important in a way that would really count. "If anyone wishes to be first..." he said, then he told them what they needed to do.

Many of us grew up with warnings about the terrible sin of pride. In our efforts to avoid pride we somehow felt that if we ever thought anything good about ourselves, we were guilty. I know what that feeling is, because for a long time I only thought negative things about myself. I thought I was being humble, but all it did was make me depressed. Jesus does not want us to go through life putting ourselves down. He wants us to be great – but he wants us to be great in the right way. He tells us what the right way is: "If anyone wants to be first, he must be last of all and the servant of all."

I'll talk about what he means by being "last" in a few moments, but first I want to say something about being a "servant." In another place in the gospels, Jesus gave an example of what it means to be a "servant" by referring to himself when he said: "The Son of Man came not to be served, but to serve." A person can be rich or poor in society, they can have many friends or few, they can be wheelers or dealers in the eyes of the world or they can be social nobodies. Being someone great in the eyes of the world is not a sin in itself, as long as we got there honestly. But God judges things differently than human beings do. To be great in God's eyes, it is not necessary for a person to be always putting themselves down or thinking of themselves as worthless. What is necessary is they have learned that the universe does not revolve around them. What is necessary is they have learned how to be servants of our God and servants of others.

I would like to comment on the example Jesus did use in today's gospel. He used a little child as an example of how his apostles were <u>supposed</u> to be. We know that children are not the most humble creatures on this earth. They can be very self-centered. In Jewish society at the time of Jesus, children were greatly loved and were seen to be a wonderful blessing from God, but they had no social standing or social power. They did not have the conceit or sophistication of adults. They knew they had much to learn, they knew they had to depend on their parents for their needs and instinctively they trusted that their needs would be met. Trust is one of the charming qualities of a child and at the same time it makes them very vulnerable. That is why it is such a terrible evil for anyone to abuse that trust.

In another place in Scripture, Jesus said: "Unless you become like little children, you cannot enter the kingdom of heaven." Jesus doesn't want us to start acting like five year olds; he doesn't want us to think we know it all but to realize we still have more to learn in life. He also doesn't want us to forget how much we depend on God as our Father, and he wants us to trust that God will meet our needs.

A child in the society of Jesus would have been last, in the sense of being at the bottom of the social ladder. Jesus said, "if anyone wishes to be first, he shall be last …" When he asks us to be last, he wants us to realize we are not too good to help others.

26th Sunday in Ordinary Time
October 1, 2006

(Numbers 11, 25-29; James 5, 1-6; Mark 9, 38-43. 45. 47-48) A few years ago, a movie came out entitled Ben Hur. Some of you might remember it. Ben Hur, whose full name was Judah Ben Hur, was played by Charlton Heston. Judah Ben Hur and his family lived well in the city of Jerusalem. Even though Israel was under the control of the Romans, the Jewish family of Ben Hur had pride, prestige and privileges. A series of misfortunes led to the loss of their privileged position and Ben Hur's mother and sister were sent to the dungeons where they eventually contracted leprosy. Judah himself was condemned to slavery and was to work in the Roman galleys. In a chain gang with other slaves, he was being marched through the countryside to his doom. On the way they paused to rest in a small village. A local man, quiet and strong, gave a cup of cold water to the exhausted prisoner, Ben Hur. Ben Hur looked up to see who was being so kind to him, and he found himself gazing into the eyes of Jesus of Nazareth. He remembered Jesus' look forever and the kind favor Jesus had done for him.

A number of years later Ben Hur won back his honor and his position. He returned to Jerusalem and to his old family house. One day, a noisy procession passed in the street as a man was jostled and pushed along to his public execution, carrying a cross. Ben Hur was filled with compassion for this prisoner, so exhausted and hardly able to walk. When the condemned criminal fell, Ben Hur moved forward to help and lift the fallen man. Their eyes met, and once again Judah Ben Hur looked into the eyes of Jesus of Nazareth. Jesus' kind action offering Ben Hur a cup of water was rewarded by the compassion Ben Hur learned to have for others who were suffering.

As Jesus passed on his way to Calvary, his shadow fell across two leper women in the crowd, the mother and sister of Judah Ben Hur. They were healed of their disease.

The story is not in the gospel but it makes a beautiful illustration of Jesus' words in today's gospel: "If anyone gives you a cup of water to drink, he will most certainly not lose his reward." The kindness of Ben Hur in running to help a fallen man was rewarded immediately through Jesus' shadow healing his mother and sister.

Jesus is telling us every good deed, even the least, will bring good things to us. God is faithful and God is not going to let us get ahead of him in being generous. Jesus reminds us also in today's gospel that every evil deed will bring us harm and that's why he warns us to get rid of evil in our lives now. He does not want us to literally cut off parts of our bodies (we would all be going around with parts missing if we did), but he is telling us even if something is near and dear to us, if it causes us to sin, we must not delay in changing things around. Fortunately when we repent of our sins, God forgets the wrong we have done. But he won't forget our good deeds.

At the time of Jesus, the villages were rather small and people could better look out for one another. In our modern world we live in a village as large as the whole world and there are so many people in need that sometimes it's overwhelming. But we can't just close our eyes and hearts and we have to help as best we can with a cup of water or a kind word.

As people struggle under their crosses, we can reach out to help them. Looking into their eyes, we may see the eyes of Jesus of Nazareth.

There will be times when we are in need of a cup of water or a kind word or a helping hand. Hopefully, someone will be there for us.

We have hundreds of opportunities to do good throughout the day. I would be remiss, however, if I did not mention a few areas here in our parish where you can do some good if you wish to. We do not hand out bottles of water as I have heard some churches do, but we provide a first class education to children, many of whom could not afford it. One of the things that enables us to do this ministry is our bingo and we're always needing helpers at our bingo. We also need coaches for sports teams, helpers at our festival, people to sing in the choir, people to visit the sick and shut-ins and to do other apostolic work through the Legion of Mary and people to help the poor through CAIN and our St. Vincent de Paul Society. Another very good thing we do here is we pray. More things are accomplished through prayer than any of us can imagine. If you want to do some good for others, here are some ideas.

Whatever good thing we do will be a blessing for

someone, but it will be a blessing for ourselves as well. Every little thing we do is important. Even if our love is not received in a grateful manner, we will not lose our reward.

27th Sunday in Ordinary Time
October 8, 2006

(Genesis 2, 18-24; Hebrews 2, 9-11; Mark 10, 2-16) The waiters and waitresses at Cinderella's Castle in Disney World treat their customers like royalty – literally. A man wrote in to Readers Digest that after lunch the waiter asked, "Is there anything else My Lord wishes?" "Yes," he said. "I'd like my wife to treat me like this at home." Then the waiter bowed to the wife and said to her "My Lord desires to be treated like a king in his castle. May I suggest a reply?" "Sure," his wife said. "Tell him he's spent too much time in Fantasyland."

Marriage brings joys and laughter, but it can also bring pain and suffering. Of course, life itself brings all these things, whether a person is married or not, but the pains and joys associated with our closest relationships touch us where we are most vulnerable. Jesus is talking to us today about those times when the joy and laughter is gone and the wife or the husband, or perhaps both, decide to call it quits.

It's always difficult to preach on this gospel without at the same time seeming to condemn those who have had to get a divorce. Sometimes there is good reason for getting a divorce. I have given my support to many people who needed to file for divorce for the legal protection it affords. Notice, as our Lord teaches that no human being has the power to separate what God has joined, he does not mention the word sin until he talks about divorce and remarriage. The Church has constantly taken Jesus' words literally even in the face of ongoing criticism for not following the liberal spirit of society today.

Everyday observation tells us the value our society places on marriage declines year by year. There are hundreds of statistics about marriage, but there are two that I think are of special significance. One is that the percent of second marriages that end in divorce is considerably higher than the percent of first marriages. This statistic shows that simply changing partners doesn't necessarily eliminate problems. The people themselves so often haven't really changed, and many of the same problems that caused the first marriage to fall apart are carried with people into a second or third relationship. That's what that statistic tells me. The second statistic is significant in that couples who live together before marriage have a slightly higher rate of divorce than couples who are more conventional and who do not live together until after they are married. This statistic destroys the assumption that it's better to test it out before tying the knot. Even those who find out what it's like to live together before they get married cannot find out what it's like to be committed to someone else until they really are committed to someone else. You can't try out the commitment of marriage until you've made the commitment. One of the many problems with society's attitude about marriage is that too many people view marriage as their own private affair. Jesus reminds us today in the quote from Genesis, that human beings didn't invent marriage. The origin of marriage is from God and God has some ideas about what marriage should be like. It's not just a private affair that allows two people to determine what the rules and regulations are. In marriage two people make a promise to each other but at the same time their promise is called a vow because that promise is also made to God. God made rules about marriage because he wants it to be a blessing for his people. And although Moses allowed divorce (which Jesus said was allowed because of the hardness of their hearts) Jesus said it was not God's plan. God's plan from the beginning was for marriage to be permanent, and although divorce is sometimes necessary, it's usually not a blessing for anyone. Evidence is building even in the scientific environment that divorce is not good either for adults or for kids. Marriage, which often is not easy, needs God's help and God will be there to help if we ask. Another item from modern day research shows that people who attend church weekly have greater marital happiness.

At a recent psychological meeting I attended, the speakers were pleading with the psychologists in the audience to get involved in helping people learn how to work out their differences and to relate with one another better, than just to break up and get a divorce. They kept insisting that divorce is more than just a legal event. It does considerable damage to all parties involved, especially the children. Children do not just bounce back after divorce, and the effects are more destructive and long lasting than what people want to recognize.

I could go on and on about this. I taught marriage in high school. I did my master's thesis in psychology on marital happiness. One conclusion I have come to is that people confuse falling in love with real love. Falling in love is wonderful, but it's only a beginning. Real love requires a certain amount of compatibility, taking time to get to know one another, it takes a lot of work, and a lot of sensitivity, understanding, forgiveness and unselfishness. When Jesus tells us the most important commandment is love, we have in that word "commandment" that it's not always going to be easy. An article I read recently surveyed couples who were unhappy in their marriages but who decided to stick it out. They reported that after five years their marriages had turned around and they were as happy as they had ever been or even happier. Today's gospel was about marriage, but whether we're married or not, we all must learn how to love. That is our calling as followers of Christ and that will be our joy in eternity.

A pastor was called to a local nursing home to perform a wedding. He was met by the anxious groom, and on meeting him the pastor started up a conversation. He asked the old man: "Do you love her?" The old man replied: "Nope." "Is she a good Christian woman?" "I don't know for sure," was the old man's answer. "Well, does she have lots of money?" asked the pastor. "I doubt it." "Then why are you marrying her?" the preacher asked. "'Cause she can drive at night," the old man said.

One of my favorite statements about marriage is this: The shortest sentence in the English language is "I am," the longest is "I do." I asked a few of my friends if they had some statements they could make about marriage that would help me with my sermon. One man said, "I better not say anything. I'm a married man." One wife said, "It depends on the day whether I'm for it or against it." One widow said, "Enjoy it while you can." Giving up marriage was the major issue I had to deal with before being ordained; and it is the major reason most people do not go into religious life or enter the priesthood.

You know, one of the things the people of Jesus' day admired <u>most</u> about Jesus was that he spoke with authority. He didn't have to quote other rabbis or give other people's opinions when giving the answer to a question. And his authority went beyond what he taught. He spoke with authority too when he healed diseases and cast out demons. One of the things modern people like <u>least</u> about him is that he spoke with authority. They would rather look upon Christ's teachings as opinions or suggestions. Especially this is true with regard to marriage. The attitude of Catholics toward marriage, divorce, sex outside of marriage, cohabitation, homosexuality, etc. is not for the most part formed by what Jesus tells us. It's pretty much formed by the attitude of society. Instead of us being a light for the world as we should be, too many of us take our light and direction from society and overlook the teachings of Christ.

One of the most difficult parts of my job is trying to convince people I have to uphold the rules the Church has about marriage. For one reason or another people often complain: "Why does the Church have all these rules? It looks like the Church is trying to make it hard for people to stay in the Church?" I have to say "I'm sorry; the Church is not trying to make it hard for people. The Church is just trying to be faithful to the teachings of Jesus about marriage." If it's meant to be permanent, why shouldn't the couple put some time into trying to prepare for it properly? If a person was married before and they don't want to bother with an annulment, they expect the Church to just throw Jesus' teaching on marriage out the window because it's too much trouble for them to follow. The Church would not be doing its job if it didn't treat marriage seriously.

When the Jews asked Jesus if it were lawful for a man to divorce his wife, they already believed they knew the answer. Divorce was permitted by Jewish law. But Jesus surprised them. He referred to the original intention God had in creating men and women. They were to provide companionship and love for one another and keep the human race going. And this drive God put in us to procreate is to be exercised in the exclusive, permanent relationship of marriage. As the Scriptures tell us, they become two in one flesh. It is based on this unique kind of union that the Church teaches and has always taught that the only appropriate expression of physical love is in marriage. Sexuality is sacred. It has to have boundaries or it will become little more than pure animal behavior. And without adequate boundaries human society will suffer and we would not be faithful to the teachings of the Scriptures.

One of the things that confuses people is the difference between annulments and divorces. A divorce is a legal matter. It is the declaration by the state that the marriage is ended. Sometimes it is necessary. Sometimes a spouse has to protect himself or herself from serious harm. But I've seen too many that were not necessary, simply because one or the other gave up too soon, or thought someone else looked more interesting. If a couple are not relating well, they can learn. I think too many people expect heaven on earth from their marriage and when it doesn't happen they look elsewhere. The Church does not grant divorces to end a marriage. The Church may grant an annulment after a marriage has broken up. An annulment is a statement that after serious investigation by Church authorities a couple are not obligated to each other under God because there was something seriously lacking in their commitment from the beginning. So often it was that one or the other person was unable or not ready at the time to make the kind of serious commitment marriage requires. It can be a very complicated process and it's best not to make rash judgments about people who could or could not get an annulment.

Part of the problem with marriage today is that it is seen by many people as a private arrangement. Its origin is from God as we heard in the first reading. In marriage two people promise God as well as each other to take each other as husband and wife "for better, for worse, for richer, for poorer, in sickness and in health until death."

I could go on talking a long time about marriage. I've worked with people before marriage. I've counseled couples who were having problems. Marital happiness was the basis for my thesis when I got my degree in psychology. In my own personal struggle with not being able to be married because of the priesthood, I've mellowed a lot. I guess that's old age. I learned that every way of life has its joys and its difficulties. Whether we're married or not, our major task in life is learning how to grow in love. That's what its all about and that will be our joy in this life and in heaven.

28th Sunday in Ordinary Time
October 15, 2006

(Wisdom 7, 7-11; Hebrews 4, 12-13; Mark 10, 17-30) "I want to tithe," a man told his pastor one day. "I want to give 10 percent of my income to church. When my income was $50 a week, I gave $5 to church every Sunday. When I was successful in business and my weekly income rose to $500 a week, I gave $50 a week. Now my income has gone to $5,000 a week, but I just can't bring myself to give $500 to the church every week." So his pastor said "why don't we pray over this?" Then the man's pastor began to pray, "Dear God, please make this man's weekly income go back down to $500 a week so he can begin to tithe again."

Tithing was a strict part of the Jewish law. It's taken for granted that the man in today's gospel was tithing faithfully, as well as conscientiously keeping all the other Jewish laws too, but he wanted to do more. Jesus offered him that opportunity. Jesus offered him the opportunity to give up everything he had for the sake of the Kingdom of God. This was an invitation that was not offered to everyone. Jesus had good friends who supported him, who must have been pretty well off to be able to do so, and he did not ask them to give up everything. The young man could not accept the invitation. It required too much of him. He wanted to do more but not that much more. What Jesus was asking wasn't impossible. Jesus himself lived a life of total poverty and his twelve apostles gave up everything in order to follow him. Though Judas, as we know, later cheated on his commitment and did not live up to it.

As we hear today's gospel, there's a temptation to think it's all about money. It is and it isn't. Money is a symbol of our lives, it represents our sweat and labor. It represents food on our table and a roof over our heads. It represents fun times. When we give money to the Church, when we give money to the poor or the missions, we are giving away part of ourselves to help someone or for some other noble purpose. It's more than just helping out where needed, it's giving back to our Lord in gratitude, in sacrifice, in humble acknowledgement of where all our blessings come from, something of ourselves. It's an innate desire built into all of us to give something of ourselves to our Creator for all that he has given to us. We call that sacrifice, and people have been doing it since human beings began to walk the face of the earth.

At the same time, the gospel is about other things than money. It's about anything that might get in the way of our giving ourselves totally to Christ. Think of all the wonderful things we have. Are they helping us on our way to God or are they getting in the way? Our ultimate purpose in life, yes, our eternal happiness, is to be with God. Are all of the things we treasure leading us there? Do we take time to thank God for them? Gratitude may lead us to be generous with our charity, but it should also lead us to be generous with our time. How much time do we make for God? Think, for example, of Sunday Mass or daily prayer. For too many people, taking time for God takes last place in their lives because they're too busy. When we're too busy for God, we really are too busy. A lot of the time, though, we're not too busy; we just don't want to put out the effort to give God some of our time. If we were to ask "what more do I need to do," Our Lord could ask us to give up some bad habit, or to let go of some grudge we keep holding onto. Maybe that's why we seldom come to him with that kind of question.

Today's first reading tells us about a person who sought wisdom before anything else. In attaining wisdom, the author of this piece from the Book of Wisdom said he acquired all things besides. St. Paul tells us Christ is the power of God and the wisdom of God. (1 Cor. 1, 24) As Jesus answered Peter in the gospel, no one who has given up everything to follow Christ will lose their reward. Indeed, they will be rewarded 100 times over. That is a fantastic return and it has been guaranteed by one who will not fail us. But he warns us that when we follow him, when we give ourselves over to him to the extent that he asks us to, life will not always go easy. One part of this process that is not always easy is simply trusting and waiting. We like immediate results but God doesn't always give them. We have to trust in God's wisdom and rely on God's timetable, but if we do, we will surely find out God will not fail us and he is not going to let us outdo him in generosity.

29th Sunday in Ordinary Time
October 22, 2006

INTRODUCTION – (Isaiah 53, 10-11; Hebrews 4, 14-16; Mark 10, 35-45) In Isaiah there are four short poems or hymns, written over 500 years before Christ, that tell us about some mysterious person or persons whose faithfulness and suffering would bring redemption to many people. The four poems are about someone God calls "my servant," thus they are called Servant Songs. Isaiah most probably had someone in mind who lived during his own time when he was writing, but these Servant Songs describe with amazing accuracy the redemptive work of Jesus Christ who lived 500 years later. All four Servant Songs are appropriately read and reflected on during Holy Week. Our first reading today is a section from the Servant Songs and is a fitting introduction to the gospel where Jesus tells us he came not to be served but to serve and to give his life as a ransom for many.

HOMILY – I have a cute story to tell. Two weeks ago, Fr. Al Bishoff came to our Oktoberfest. The following week in his homily he happened to mention that he was here and had a delicious brat and sauerkraut sandwich. How he fit that in with his homily, I don't know, but sometime after having preached it, a parishioner came to him and said that was one of his best and most inspiring homilies. Right after Mass, she told him, I was inspired to go out and buy a brat and sauerkraut sandwich. Here he thought she was complimenting him for giving such a great homily. I guess she popped his bubble. He commented, "You never know what some people are going to be impressed by when you get up to talk."

We all have our pride deflated from time to time and it helps keep us humble. One more story but not as close to home. At a big multimillion dollar company all the secretaries had gone home, so the big CEO of the company stood by the shredding machine with a paper in his hand looking very confused. A janitor saw him there and offered to help. The boss said "This paper's extremely important. Can you get this thing to work?" The janitor turned the machine on, took the paper and fed it in. "Thanks," said the CEO. "I just need one copy!"

Jesus burst the bubble of James and John today when they came up to him asking to be put into the top jobs when Jesus took over running the country as they expected he would! He had just warned them for the third time about the suffering and death he was soon to face and they still didn't get it. He must have felt really frustrated and isolated at times. It's a wonder Jesus didn't just scream out "I don't know how to get through to you guys." But with amazing gentleness he told James and John they didn't understand what they were asking. Could they go through what he would have to go through? With enthusiasm they said they certainly could. He warned them, they would. Then he made it clear to them, as he had previously, there's nothing wrong with wanting to be great. Greatness in God's eyes is not the same as what the world considers greatness. Greatness from God's viewpoint is service to others. This is something anyone can do, from a child helping at home to a clerk in the supermarket, to the president of a large corporation.

Being a servant does not mean having people walk all over us. A policeman who didn't stop reckless drivers wouldn't be serving anyone. A parent who let their child do whatever they want wouldn't be serving their child. A teacher who would let a student get by with cheating or not doing their work would be a poor servant as well as a poor teacher. Being a servant is not always easy and often not popular. Jesus knew that. Yet he still came to serve, by healing, by teaching the truth, even though it created enemies for him. He was ready to sacrifice his life to continue serving, even when people ignored him or hated him.

I would like to comment briefly on the last words in today's gospel: that Jesus came to give his life as "a ransom for many." Two words are important here: the word "many" and the word "ransom." 1) I think the word "many" implies there are some who are not saved because they have chosen a path that leads to eternal unhappiness rather than to eternal life. This word seems to fly in the face of the so called new age theology which supposes there will be no hell and everyone, no matter how they lived, will end up enjoying the blessedness of heaven. If everyone is going to be saved, why did Christ waste his time trying to point out to us how we are to live and what we must do in order to enter into eternal life? 2) This word "ransom" is a word that connects with customs that were practiced many centuries ago. In olden times slaves or captives or prisoners were ransomed, but it seldom happens today. I want to end with a modern day story that might convey the idea of "ransom." It's about St. Maximilian Kolbe who understood and lived the spirit of Jesus, the spirit of service. He gave his life as a ransom for another.

Maximilian was a priest and was twice arrested by the Nazis during the second world war for his religious activities. The second time he ended up in Auschwitz. A prisoner in the jail there escaped and the commandant punished the entire prison camp by announcing that ten prisoners would die by starvation. The commandant walked along the ranks relishing this chance to choose the ten men for death. As the ten he chose were being marched off to the starvation bunkers, Maximilian broke rank with the other prisoners, walked up to one of the ten men who were marching to their death and said, "I would like to take that man's place. He has a wife and children." The surprised commandant kicked the man out of line and allowed Maximilian to take his place in the death march. He was starved for days before the Nazis got tired of waiting for him to die. So they sent an SS officer to give him an injection of carbolic acid to kill him.

We celebrate now the love of One who gave his life as a ransom for all of us.

30th Sunday in Ordinary Time
October 29, 2006

INTRODUCTION – (Jeremiah 31, 7-9; Hebrews 5, 1-6; Mark 10, 46-52) The Jews have had numerous periods of great suffering throughout history. One of those difficult periods was during the Babylonian exile. The prophet who speaks to us in today's first reading, Jeremiah, lived through it all. Before the exile he had the unpopular task of telling God's people what they needed to do in order to avoid disaster – unpopular because he had to tell them they had to start obeying God's laws. Instead of heeding his counsel the people tried to kill Jeremiah. When the Babylonians descended upon Judah, they took many people captive as slaves to Babylon. Jeremiah could have said "I told you so." But he didn't. Instead he offered God's people hope. We hear him in today's first reading telling a conquered people: "shout for joy for Jacob" for God would bring his people back home. Even the blind and the lame would not be left behind. The passage prepares us for the gospel where Jesus heals a blind man.

HOMILY – Jericho is a pretty little city near where the Jordan river meets the Dead Sea. It is perhaps the oldest city in the entire world and the lowest. It is almost 1300 feet below sea level, whereas Death Valley, the lowest point in the western hemisphere is a mere 282 feet below sea level. On a map Jerusalem and Jericho are only about 15 miles apart, but the trip from Jericho to Jerusalem would be all up hill, for you see, Jerusalem is over 2300 feet above sea level. At any rate, our gospel tells us Jesus was leaving Jericho. It doesn't tell us where he was going. But the very next paragraph in our bible tells us his next stop was Jerusalem where he would enter the Temple in grand triumph on the following Sunday, Palm Sunday. Six days later he would die on a cross. Prophetically, Bartimaeus anticipated the praise Jesus would receive in Jerusalem when he addresses Jesus as "Son of David," a royal title.

When Jesus healed him he told him "go your way." Bartimaeus instead went Jesus' way. St. Mark tells us he followed him "on the way." St. Mark implies it was on the way that Jesus was going. It took as much faith to do that as to be healed, I suppose, because he didn't know where Jesus was headed and what was ahead. Isn't that true of us? We wish to follow Jesus, but we're never quite sure (and even sometimes apprehensive as to) where he's going to take us. Maybe that's why so many people hesitate to follow him too closely. After all, didn't he say "if anyone would come after me, let him take up his cross and follow me?" Like James and John in last week's gospel who asked to sit at Jesus' right and left when he entered into his glory, we want to reign with him, but we're not too keen about dying with him.

Jesus spent his whole life trying to heal blindness – primarily blindness in our minds and hearts: the blindness of our prejudices, our unforgiveness, our selfishness and self centeredness, our criticism of others without seeing our own faults, even our blindness to our own good qualities, just to name a few examples.

One form of blindness is the blindness of unbelief in Jesus' death and resurrection. "What?" You say. "We believe in Jesus' death and resurrection. We show our faith in it by coming to Mass. We profess it every time we say the creed." That's true, but that's only half the story. The other half comes when we can apply it to our lives, trusting that when we faithfully follow him, even out of our own crosses Christ can bring resurrection and life. As St. Paul told us "We know that all things work for good for those who love God." (Rom. 8, 28) Can we believe that when we lose someone we love, when we see ourselves growing older or more infirm, when we have to say good by to some of our fondest dreams, when the people or the world around us changes in ways we do not like? Now, don't misunderstand me. I'm not promoting needless suffering. When I'm sick I call a doctor. But we all face tragic situations about which nothing can be done. Do we then retreat into bitterness, resentment, despair or do we choose to live in the faith and hope of God's ability to bring life out of death? Are we willing to follow Jesus to Calvary so we can experience resurrection? Imprisoned by our many blind spots, often we, like Bartimaeus, sit by the side of the road of life begging for whatever goodies this world will throw our way. Are we able to pray today with Bartimaeus, "Teacher, I want to see," so I can follower you better for you are the way? Amen.

All Saints
November 1, 2006

INTRODUCTION – (Rev 7, 2-4. 9-14; 1 John 3, 1-3; Matthew 5, 1-12a) Our first reading is from the book of Revelation. The section just preceding today's passage described the end of the world. The sun became dark and the moon became red as blood and there was a great earthquake all over the earth. People tried to hide from all these terrible things and they asked: "Who can survive?" Today's reading answers the question: those who have followed Christ faithfully. The book tells us 144,000 are to be saved. We do not take that number literally. It is a symbolic number, symbolic of perfection. Notice after it refers to the number 144,000 it speaks of those who are saved as such a large crowd that no one could count them.

HOMILY – Just two and a half weeks ago, the Holy Father canonized several new saints, among them was a saint who lived and worked here in the United States. I was deeply impressed when I recently read about her in the latest St. Anthony Messenger. Her name is St. Theodora Guérin. I would like to tell you a little about her. St. Theodora was born in France in 1798. When she was 15 years old her father was killed and her mother went into a deep depression, so severe that she could no longer function or care for her two daughters, Theodora and Theodora's younger sister. Theodora had to take over running the house and caring for her mother and her sister. Although Theodora wanted to enter the convent at age 20, her mother could not bear to lose her and Theodora had to wait until she was 25 until her mother was strong enough for Theodora to leave home. She became a Sister of Providence. Her early years were spent as a teacher and as superior of other sisters in her community. She was happy doing these jobs, but her Mother Superior convinced her to go to the United States as a missionary. She was not eager to travel from her home in France and her health was fragile. But she promised obedience to do what she was asked to do so she went. Remember this was back in 1839.

Just to give you a sense of what she was getting into, just think of Cincinnati at that time. Travel was difficult. There were no highways, no bridges between Cincinnati and Covington. There were not more than about a dozen or two homes in Northside and Indians still roamed through the area. There was only one church in Cincinnati in 1839, the Cathedral downtown. A couple of more were soon to start. And this was the Queen City of the West. So you can imagine what a wilderness western Indiana must have been, which is where St. Theodora was to settle. Her trip across the Atlantic Ocean, by ship of course, took several months. It was a trip in which their ship was almost destroyed several times by hurricanes and severe storms. But eventually she and five other sisters arrived in one piece in New York. No one was there to meet them and they didn't speak English. Somehow though, they managed to find places to stay and eventually, traveling by train, stagecoach, and steamboat, they reached Madison, Indiana. The bishop there, whose diocese included all of Indiana and part of Illinois, sent them north toward Terre Haute where he wanted them to work. Their stagecoach ride involved traveling through thick forests on non-existent roads, having the stagecoach overturn and their being thrown out, crossing rivers where there were no bridges, and eventually, when they were in the middle of a dense forest, their guide stopped the stagecoach and said this is where you are going to live. And they did. Their years there involved living in a log cabin, surviving for days without food, times of sickness, hot summers and cold winters and having their crops and cattle destroyed by fire. They started a school for girls with ten girls, now known as Saint Mary-of-the-Woods College. In addition to the physical stresses they had to endure, her bishop was a royal pain. Eventually Rome asked him to retire because other missionaries were having such a hard time dealing with him. Having survived all that for 15 years, St. Theodora saw her sisters grow from six to 60 and the number of students she and her sisters were teaching increased from ten to 1,200. St. Theodora died at the age of 57 on May 14, 1856. It is impressive to think of the sacrifices people have made to build this country and to plant the seeds of faith and to think how we have benefited from their spirit and their love and dedication.

Today is the feast of All Saints. I told you about one saint. I'm sure there were hundreds of thousands like St. Theodora through the past 2000 years. I'm sure there were many whose names we don't know and whose names we never will know. I am sure among those holy people who preceded us were parents, grandparents, great grandparents, uncles and aunts who lived their faith with devotion, who made great sacrifices for their families and who passed their values and beliefs on to their children. Today we honor all of them. May we faithfully follow our Lord and pass on to others the values and beliefs we have been blessed with and one day share in the eternal happiness they now enjoy. Amen.

31st Sunday in Ordinary Time
November 5, 2006

(Dt. 6, 2-6; Hebrews 7, 23-28; Mark 12, 28b-34) The rabbis and Jewish religious leaders at the time of Jesus would often discuss which of their 613 laws was the most important. They asked Jesus' opinion and as usual Jesus got right to the heart of the matter. Jesus was not saying the others do not count or are unimportant. He was saying that love is the spirit behind all of them. If we follow the command of love, we will keep the others, if we keep the others without love we are legalists or as Paul says in his famous 13th chapter of I Corinthians "If I have not love, I am nothing." Jesus was asked for one commandment, but he gave us two, to show that the two are inseparable. Part of the problems people have in today's world is that they have forgotten the first part of this commandment. That's why they have problems with the second. It's interesting too to notice the word "commandment." It reminds us that we don't always feel love for God or for others, but we are obliged to do it anyway if we are going to fulfill our highest potential as a human being and if we are going to please God.

I was going to bring with me today all the books I have that have the word "love" in the title. But there were too many to bring. So, just think of a big stack of books up here. My purpose in mentioning there are so many books is to illustrate that love can be very complex and learning to love God and others is not always as easy as we would like to think that it is. In is interesting that the English language, which has a plentitude of words, relies so heavily on the one word "love" to mean so many things. Even the Greek language, which was rather primitive, had three words for the word love, depending on the kind of love that was being spoken of. We use the one word "love" to describe everything from a score in tennis to the most selfish, lustful cravings to the most sublime and unselfish act of kindness toward another. For this reason it is a challenge to talk about and a challenge to put into practice.

The biggest misconception about love in today's world is to equate it with feelings. Too many people think love means having nice warm, friendly feelings toward someone. Well, it is and it isn't. Love is an emotion, but the kind of love Jesus is talking about is much more. Warm feelings don't always feed the hungry or help a person in need. Love is not primarily something vague, fuzzy and warm. Love is a matter of what one does rather than what one feels.

One of the Peanuts' cartoons had Linus telling his sister Lucy that he wanted to be a doctor when he grew up. Lucy responded in her usual cynical fashion by saying "You, a doctor? That's a laugh. You know why you couldn't be a doctor? Because you don't love humankind." Linus thought about this for a moment then said "I do love humankind. It's people I can't stand." It's easy to have nice warm, happy feelings of love for vague humanity, or even for a God who will do for us whatever we want him to do. But where are those nice warm happy feelings when a parent has to get up in the middle of the night to care for a crying baby or when an adult child has to care for an aging parent or even when God commands things we don't want to do. When we do the right thing, that's love at work also.

There is a beautiful story in Chicken Soup for the Soul about a little girl who was dying of a very rare disease. Her only hope for survival was to get a blood transfusion from her five year old brother who had survived the same disease and whose body had developed antibodies needed to combat the illness. The doctor explained to the little boy what a transfusion was and asked if he would be willing to give blood to his sister. He hesitated for a moment then said "yes, if it will save Lisa." As the transfusion progressed he lay in bed next to his sister and smiled, along with all the medical staff, as they saw color return to Lisa's cheeks. Then the little boy's smile faded and with a very serious look on his face and a trembling voice he asked the doctor "Will I start to die now?" The boy had misunderstood the doctor and thought he would have to give his sister all his blood. Love is not always a happy, painless, easy, carefree thing. Love, when it is real love, requires unselfishness and that's not always easy, especially when it is required of us over long periods of time.

Love has some difficult elements to it such as sacrifice and unselfishness. You know, when we are born we're pretty self centered creatures. We know when we're hungry, when we're in pain, when we're tired and we don't mind letting the whole world know about it. That's OK for a baby. But we're supposed to grow out of that stage and realize we're not the center of the universe. When we grow in love we are learning to reach out to others and this is a sign of maturity.

A word about love for God. Feelings enter in here too and when they're not present people become confused. When they don't get good feelings from prayer or Mass they often feel they are losing their faith or God has abandoned them or they just quit trying.

Sometimes our love for God produces good feelings, but love for God is not measured by how we feel. Basically, love for God is a matter of giving God our trust, our time and our obedience. Jesus gave us a reliable measure of our love for God when he told us: "If you love me you will keep my commandments."

We come together today to offer God our worship and our love. As we recall Jesus unselfish love for us in giving his life for us on the cross, we ask him to help us learn the true meaning of love. Amen.

32nd Sunday in Ordinary Time
November 12, 2006

INTRODUCTION – (1 Kings 17, 10-16; Hebrews 9, 24-28; Mark 12, 38-44) I want to begin by saying something about the second reading. The author of the Letter to the Hebrews was interested in showing the superiority of Jesus' sacrifice to those of the Old Testament. He is presuming those who received this letter would be thinking of the once a year sacrifice on the Day of Atonement (Yom Kippur) which was just celebrated a few weeks ago on October 2. In the days before the Temple was destroyed by the Romans, the High Priest would enter the Holy Place, where no one ever went except on this occasion and he would offer sacrifice for the sins of God's people. The Letter to the Hebrews emphasizes that Christ's sacrifice for sins took place only once and didn't need to be offered again and again because his sacrifice was perfect.

Our first reading will make more sense if we know that the events that are described in the reading happened during a severe famine. We have to marvel at the faith of this widow.

HOMILY – Humans have offered sacrifices to their gods since the dawn of history and before. Human beings have sensed that someone higher and greater than we are put us here and that someone has a hand in our destiny. Up until the era of the Jews, with one very brief exception, all peoples believed that someone was a multitude of powerful beings they called gods. Sacrifice was a way to maintain communion with these gods, especially a way of acknowledging our dependence on them and seeking to win their favor. Sacrifices were gifts to the deity that represented the giver and were usually something that symbolized the life of the person offering the sacrifice. That's why food, animals used for food, and blood were usually offered. Some people even offered their own children as sacrifice.

We read in the gospels that Jesus was a pious Jew. He observed the Sabbath, he went to Jerusalem for the feasts, he celebrated the Passover. His life itself was a sacrifice in that he served his Father perfectly through prayer and by his ministry of teaching and healing. His ministry got him into trouble with the powerful political and religious leaders of his day and, because he was faithful to it, in their eyes he had to be destroyed. It was in perfect love he gave himself. The Letters to the Hebrews tells us he only needed to die once, and we can tap into the power of his saving love through the Eucharist. To communicate with our God, to acknowledge our dependence on him, to seek his favor, we no longer need to offer food and animals to represent ourselves. We can offer our love through a perfect sacrifice, for through the Mass we unite ourselves with Christ's sacrifice and we offer ourselves to the Father.

That sacrifice will bring great blessings back to us. The widow of Zarephath made a sacrifice of what she had to feed God's prophet and God blessed her with a continuous supply of food. Then there's the woman in the gospel. There were a number of receptacles in the Temple area where people dropped in their offerings. Money was always in the form of precious metal, so when it was dropped into the receptacles it made enough noise that bystanders could guess whether it was a large sum or small. Can't you see this poor lady following a wealthy scribe whose donation made quite a loud noise (clang, clang, clang, clang) and hers just a couple of very tiny clinks. An ordinary person would have been impressed with the large donations, but Jesus could look into hearts and he knew what her sacrifice cost her. The widow in the gospel won Jesus' overwhelming approval and most probably many blessings we do not know about.

Several years ago I visited the Twin Towers in New York. One particular exhibit struck me. It was describing how people evolved from being hunters and gatherers to the development of agriculture. The exhibit speculated that our early ancestors who were hunters and gatherers would offer their customary sacrifices of grain they had gathered in the woods and fields and sprinkle the grain around their sacred monuments or idols. Someone discovered that grain grew more abundantly in their sacred areas and it suddenly dawned on them there was a connection between throwing the seed in that area and an abundance of grain in return. I thought, of course, the more we give God the more God will bless us. People discovered it with grain, but I believe it's true of everything. Giving God time, money (to charity), our talents, our love will come back in abundant blessings. The bible has always told us that: "He who sows sparingly will reap sparingly, he who sows bountifully will reap bountifully."

Today we are about to offer the perfect sacrifice to our Creator and Father. May our hearts overflow with love and gratitude and may God bless all of us. Amen.

33rd Sunday in Ordinary Time
November 19, 2006

INTRODUCTION – (Daniel 12, 1-3; Hebrews 10, 11-14. 18; Mark 13, 24-32) The Greek word "apocalypsis" means revealing something or making something fully known. There are many passages in the Bible that are apocalyptic in nature. Most were written during a time when God's people were being persecuted. They gave hope to God's people during those times that if they remained faithful to God they would be victorious in the end. The last book of the Bible is called the Book of Revelation. It is also called the Apocalypse because that is the word with which the book begins. Today we hear another example of apocalyptic writing in the Book of Daniel. Today's first reading was composed about 165 years before Christ during the time when the Syrians were trying to obliterate the Jewish religion. During this painful historical time, any books from the Hebrew Scriptures that could be found were burned, the temple was turned into a temple to the Greek god, Zeus, and any Jews who refused to offer sacrifice to pagan gods were put to death. This passage contains a clear belief in the resurrection of the body by the year 165 BC.

HOMILY – There was an old monk dying in a little country monastery. The monks living with him knew he was dying and so they tried to make him as comfortable as possible. One of the things they did for him was to give him a little warm milk each day with a little brandy mixed into it. This seemed to calm him down. When he was getting ready to breathe his last, they asked him if he had any last words for them. He said: "brothers, whatever you do, don't ever get rid of that cow."

There was a funeral director who regularly ended his letters with the words: "Eventually yours."

We're all headed toward that day when we're going to meet our maker. It's a time very few people, especially those who are younger, care to hear about or think about. But as the year comes to an end, the Church takes this occasion to make us aware that our life in this world will come to an end someday too. Or as one of my friends often says: "everything has a beginning, a middle and an end." In reminding us of these things, the Church is not trying to depress us. It is trying to keep us in touch with reality. The reality is God has better plans for us than for us to spend a few short years in this life, and then for that to be the end for us. "You are my inheritance, O Lord" is our psalm refrain. In other words, God created us to be with him. God showed us through his Son the way to get there.

I explained earlier that our first reading was an example of apocalyptic writing giving the Jews hope as they suffered through a time of great persecution. The passage today from St. Mark's gospel is also an example of apocalyptic writing. Mark's gospel was written during the early Christian persecutions. Like all apocalyptic writing it tells us the time of suffering will be short and those who are faithful to God will emerge victorious.

We know time is relative. Christmas will be here in a little more than a month. Most of us are running around frantically thinking how can it come so quickly. For a six year old child, it probably seems like it will never get here. To say the time of suffering will be short is relative. How short is short? Sometimes when we're suffering it seems to go on forever and we get discouraged. Compared to eternity, though, it will be very short. In the meantime, we have the sacraments and Jesus' word to sustain us. His words will never pass away. It is our sure rock.

Jesus' statement that "This generation will not pass away until all these things have taken place" is a confusing one. Earlier in this chapter from Mark, Jesus had been talking about the destruction of the Temple and some of his thoughts about that catastrophic event got mixed in with his prediction of his second coming. I'm sure in the minds of the early Christians the end of the Temple and of Jerusalem would have been happening at the same time that the world was coming to an end, and then Jesus would come the second time in glory. There is something else Jesus said that indicates the second coming would not happen in the near future. He said that when he came the second time in glory he would gather his elect from the ends of the earth. Jesus' words would not spread to the ends of the earth for a number of centuries.

Tribulation and suffering will not last forever and if we are faithful to the Lord, he will bring us into a springtime of new life that will never end. We must not let anything discourage us, but keep watch and be ready for we do not know when the Lord will tell us he's ready for us.

(*I skipped this in later Masses and added some of these thoughts in an adlibbed fashion to the second last paragraph:* In St. Mark's gospel, two events are confused with one another: the destruction of Jerusalem and the Temple, on the one hand, and on the other hand, the end of the world along with Jesus' second coming. Mark was writing to a people who expected it to happen all at the same time and that it would happen very soon. Several times in the gospels, Jesus warned his followers they would risk suffering and death if they were loyal to him. By the time Mark was writing, the early Church was experiencing first hand what Jesus prophesized. Peter and Paul probably had been put to death by this time. The apocalyptic message in today's gospel sounds gloomy and foreboding, but if we look at it closer it proclaims good news: The Son of Man will come to rescue his people. He will gather them from the four corners of the earth to himself. Jesus tells us just as the branches of the fig tree starting to grow green and tender is a sign that winter is over, so when trouble and suffering come upon us, know that it will soon be over and spring will come. And it will be a springtime bringing new life that will go on forever. In the verses just before and right after our gospel Jesus tells his followers to be on guard, be alert. We never know when any of these things will happen.)

Thanksgiving
November 23, 2006

(Sir 50, 22-24; 1 Cor 1, 3-9; Luke 17, 11-19) It seems redundant to offer a Mass in Thanksgiving. That's what every Mass is. The central part of the Mass is introduced with the words "Let us give thanks to the Lord our God." Surely, the Mass includes many other themes at times, it is prayer of praise, it is prayer of petition, it is a prayer for someone who has died, it is a reminder of Jesus death and resurrection, it is a vehicle for preaching the gospel. In every instance though, it is a way to tell God thanks, thanks for his love, thanks for his blessings, thanks for all that he has done for us in

Jesus, thanks for the faith and hope that we have. Every day, certainly every Sunday, we are called to give remember and thanks. In our day with so large a number of people finding it too inconvenient to get to Mass on Sunday, I wonder whether they have forgotten that the Mass is our great prayer of thanks have, or whether they have just forgotten to be grateful.

Sure, most of us have worked for what we have. But we forget that if it weren't for the health, the intelligence, the opportunities, the work skills and values we have been given, we would not have been able to accomplish much. We forget. And so we are reminded. We are reminded by a tradition that goes all the way back to 1622 by a colony of settlers who where glad to have survived during that year. They had lost half of their colony the previous winter. This tradition was made a national holiday during another difficult time, 1863. It was the third year of the civil war. It is unfair to say this of everyone, but it seems sometimes that the more we human beings are given, the less grateful we become. We are reminded by our faith that Thanksgiving is an attitude, an attitude that we are to carry with us all the time. As we hear St. Paul tell us today: "dedicate yourselves to thankfulness." It is an attitude that is a basic part of our personalities. It comes from humility – knowing that we are indebted to the goodness of our Creator. It leads to joy. If you want to find joy, start being grateful. A person who is always wanting more or who is never satisfied, a person who thinks the world owes him a living, that person will never find joy. It is only when we know how blessed we are that we will begin to experience joy, but we will only know how blessed we are when we start cultivating the virtue of gratitude. I will end with a story: Chicken Soup, vol., 3 pg. 205.

Feast of Christ the King
November 26, 2006

INTRODUCTION – (Daniel 7, 13-14; Rev. 1, 5-8; John 18, 33b-37) Today again we hear from the book of Daniel, a book that was written during a time when the Jews were suffering a terrible persecution for their faith. Today's reading describes how God would triumph in the end. God would establish a kingdom that would be everlasting. God is here described as "the Ancient One." His kingdom would be ruled by one who is described as "like a son of man." God would give this "son of man" dominion, glory and kingship. The term "son of man" simply means a human being, but today's passage invests the term with new depth and mystery. You might recall, "son of man" was the favorite term Jesus used to describe himself.

HOMILY – You may be surprised to know that today's feast was not established during the Middle Ages when most of the world was ruled by kings or emperors. Today's feast is very recent. It was established by Pope Pius XI in 1925, a time when kings and emperors were becoming increasingly a remnant of the past. Pius XI instituted this feast as an attempt to counteract the atheism and secularism of that time.

Today's feast reminds us that with God there is no democracy. It pleased God to establish a kingdom with Jesus his divine Son as our king. In many ways he is unlike most of the other kings we may have heard of or read about. I would like to mention just four of the things that are unique about Jesus as a king:

(1) First of all, belonging to his kingdom is intentional. He doesn't come around with soldiers and weapons to force us into submission. He <u>invites</u> us to

follow him. Coercion is not his style, rather he leads us by faith and love.

(2) As a king he does not live in a castle or go parading around in fancy garb or expensive jewels or need to be transported in big limousines or private jets. He does not need to display his position for his dignity and greatness are beyond this world. We see him in today's gospel, looking like the bad guy, on trial for violation of Jewish and Roman law. Yet it seems Pilate is the one on trial, not knowing how to honestly deal with this man in front of him. Hearing this passage we realize we are on trial too as to whether we belong to the truth for he said: "Everyone who belongs to the truth listens to my voice."

(3) Kings tend to be distant and aloof from their people. They can't be otherwise, because they have so many people to govern. Jesus, as our king, is close to each of us; not only close to us but he is one with us. "Whoever loves me will keep my word, and my Father will love him, and we will come to him and make our dwelling with him." (Jn. 14,23) He is the shepherd who seeks out the lost sheep, because each of us is important to him.

(4) Every king will enjoy his position of authority only for a time. It may be many decades, such as Louis XIV who reigned for 72 years in France, or it may be a few days until death or a rival overthrows them. Christ's kingdom will last forever.

As any king he gives us laws which he expects us to follow. The obedience he demands is not for his own self-interest but for our well being. He knows what will result in our happiness or unhappiness, so he commands us to do those things that will bring us happiness - not just momentary happiness (which sometimes sin brings us), but eternal happiness.

Kings, indeed any ruling power, requires those that are governed to pay taxes. How else can a government survive? Even God has taxes. In the Old Testament, God required 10% be given to the Lord and to the poor. Jesus too asks us to help each other, especially those who are needy among us. But there's something equally important we must give to the Lord: our time. People have to spend time together for any relationship to begin, be sustained or survive. One minimum requirement he gave us is that we give God an hour on Sunday (or Saturday evening). But that is a minimum. If we want our relationship with God to grow, we need more than that.

Our feast today reminds us there is a power in this universe that is greater than the power of physical strength, the power of hatred, the power of wealth and the power of bombs. It is the power of truth and love. This power is revealed to us in Jesus Christ. The power of Jesus Christ will overcome all the powers of evil. There may be challenging and difficult times. We may wonder where our world is headed. We may be worried about Iran, North Korea, terrorists, Iraq. We may think, and rightly so, that morality is going down the sewer. Yet, in the big picture, evil will not win out. Returning to our first reading we heard that to the Son of Man was given dominion, glory, and kingship; all peoples, nations and languages would serve him. His dominion is an everlasting dominion that shall not be taken away, his kingship shall not be destroyed. Amen.

A Priest Is a Gift from God

by Rita Ring

REFRAIN

C   F   C   Am   C

A priest is a gift from God. A priest is a gift from God.

F   C   F   G

This is My Bod - y, This is My Blood, A

VERSES 1, 3

C   F   C   C   F   G

priest is a gift from God.
1. Come to Me, My chil - dren,
3. Come to Me, chil-dren of God,

C   F   G   C   F   G

I want to pos-sess your soul, I love you so ten - der - ly,
I want to pos-sess your soul, I give My-self to ___ you

C   F   G   C   F   C

I want you to love Me too, A priest is a gift from God.
in the Ho - ly Eu-cha-rist, A priest is a gift from God.

F   G   C   F   C

I tell you My chil - dren, a priest is a gift from God. To -
I tell you My chil - dren, a priest is a gift from God. To -

F   G   C   F   G

day is the day the Lord has made, Wake, My chil-dren from your sleep,
day is the day the Lord has made, Wake, My chil-dren from your sleep,

Come My chil-dren to My al-tar,____ A
Come My chil-dren to My al-tar,____ A

VERSE 2

priest is a gift from God.   2. Come to Me, My lit-tle chil-dren,
priest is a gift from God.

I want to pos-sess your soul.   Give your hearts to Je-sus and Mar-y,

You will be one in Our Hearts, A   priest is a gift from God.

Of-fer sac-ri-fice My chil-dren, A   priest is a gift from God.

One in your heart, one in your mind, one__ in this ho-ly ban-quet,

Come My chil-dren to My al-tar, A   priest is a gift from God.

How to Become a
Shepherd of Christ Associate

The Shepherds of Christ has prayer chapters all over the world praying for the priests, the Church and the world. These prayers that Father Carter compiled in the summer of 1994 began this worldwide network of prayer. Currently the prayers are in six languages with the Church's Imprimatur. Fr. Carter had the approval of his Jesuit provincial for this movement, writing the Newsletter every 2 months for 6 1/2 years.  After his death, and with his direction, we in the Shepherds of Christ circulated the Priestly Newsletter Book II to 95,000 priests with other writings. We have prayed daily for the priests, the Church, and the world since 1994. Associates are called to join prayer Chapters and help us circulate this newsletter centered on spreading devotion to the Sacred Heart and Immaculate Heart and helping to renew the Church through greater holiness. Please form a Prayer Chapter & order a Prayer Manual.

Apostles of the Eucharistic Heart of Jesus

The Shepherds of Christ have people dedicated to spending two hours weekly before the Blessed Sacrament in the Tabernacle. They pray for the following intentions:

1) For the spread of the devotion to the Hearts of Jesus and Mary culminating in the reign of the Sacred Heart and the triumph of the Immaculate Heart.
2) For the Pope.
3) For all bishops of the world.
4) For all priests.
5) For all sisters and brothers in religious life.
6) For all members of the Shepherds of Christ Movement, and for the spread of this movement to the world.
7) For all members of the Catholic Church.
8) For all members of the human family.
9) For all souls in purgatory.

This movement, ***Apostles of the Eucharistic Heart of Jesus***, was began with Fr. Carter. Please inquire. Shepherds of Christ Ministries P.O. Box 627, China, Indiana 47250 USA or info@sofc.org

Prayer for Union with Jesus

Come to me, Lord, and possess my soul. Come into my heart and permeate my soul. Help me to sit in silence with You and let You work in my heart.

I am Yours to possess. I am Yours to use. I want to be selfless and only exist in You. Help me to spoon out all that is me and be an empty vessel ready to be filled by You. Help me to die to myself and live only for You. Use me as You will. Let me never draw my attention back to myself. I only want to operate as You do, dwelling within me.

I am Yours, Lord. I want to have my life in You. I want to do the will of the Father. Give me the strength to put aside the world and let You operate my very being. Help me to act as You desire. Strengthen me against the distractions of the devil to take me from Your work.

When I worry, I have taken my focus off of You and placed it on myself. Help me not to give in to the promptings of others to change what in my heart You are making very clear to me. I worship You, I adore You and I love You. Come and dwell in me now.

Prayer Before the
Holy Sacrifice of the Mass

Let me be a holy sacrifice and unite with God in the sacrament of His greatest love.

I want to be one in Him in this act of love, where He gives Himself to me and I give myself as a sacrifice to Him. Let me be a holy sacrifice as I become one with Him in this my act of greatest love to Him.

Let me unite with Him more, that I may more deeply love Him. May I help make reparation to His adorable Heart and the heart of His Mother, Mary. With greatest love, I offer myself to You and pray that You will accept my sacrifice of greatest love. I give myself to You and unite in Your gift of Yourself to me. Come and possess my soul.

Cleanse me, strengthen me, heal me. Dear Holy Spirit act in the heart of Mary to make me more and more like Jesus.

Father, I offer this my sacrifice, myself united to Jesus in the Holy Spirit to You. Help me to love God more deeply in this act of my greatest love.

Give me the grace to grow in my knowledge, love and service of You and for this to be my greatest participation in the Mass. Give me the greatest graces to love You so deeply in this Mass, You who are so worthy of my love.

Father Carter requested
that these be prayed in prayer
chapters all over the world.

Shepherds of Christ

Prayers

Shepherds of Christ Associates

PRAYER MANUAL

Shepherds of Christ Publications
China, Indiana

Imprimi Potest: Rev. Bradley M. Schaeffer, S.J.
Provincial
Chicago Province, The Society of Jesus

Imprimatur: Most Rev. Carl K. Moeddel
Auxiliary Bishop
Archdiocese of Cincinnati

The Shepherds of Christ Associates Prayer Manual is published by
Shepherds of Christ Publications, an arm of Shepherds of Christ Ministries,
P.O. Box 627 China, Indiana 47250 USA.

Founder, Shepherds of Christ Ministries:
Father Edward J. Carter, S.J.

For more information contact:
Shepherds of Christ Associates
P.O. Box 627
China, Indiana 47250- USA
Tel. 812-273-8405
Toll Free: 1-888-211-3041
Fax 812-273-3182

Chapter Meeting
Prayer Format

The prayer format below should be followed at chapter meetings of *Shepherds of Christ Associates*. All prayers, not just those said specifically for priests, should include the intention of praying for all the needs of priests the world over.

1. **Hymns.** Hymns may be sung at any point of the prayer part of the meeting.

2. **Holy Spirit Prayer.** Come, Holy Spirit, almighty Sanctifier, God of love, who filled the Virgin Mary with grace, who wonderfully changed the hearts of the apostles, who endowed all Your martyrs with miraculous courage, come and sanctify us. Enlighten our minds, strengthen our wills, purify our consciences, rectify our judgment, set our hearts on fire, and preserve us from the misfortunes of resisting Your inspirations. Amen.

3. **The Rosary.**

4. **Salve Regina.** "Hail Holy Queen, Mother of mercy, our life, our sweetness, and our hope. To you do we cry, poor banished children of Eve. To you do we send up our sighs, our mourning, our weeping in this vale of tears. Turn, then, most gracious advocate, your eyes of mercy toward us and after this, our exile, show unto us the blessed fruit of your womb, Jesus, O clement, O loving, O sweet Virgin Mary. Amen."

5. **The Memorare.** "Remember, O most gracious Virgin Mary, that never was it known that anyone who fled to your protection, implored your help, or sought your intercession was left unaided. Inspired by this confidence, I fly unto you, O Virgin of virgins, my Mother. To you I come, before you I stand, sinful and

sorrowful. O Mother of the Word Incarnate, despise not my petitions, but, in your mercy, hear and answer me. Amen."

6. **Seven Hail Marys in honor of the Seven Sorrows of Mary.** Mary has promised very special graces to those who do this on a daily basis. Included in the promises of Our Lady for those who practice this devotion is her pledge to give special assistance at the hour of death, including the sight of her face. The seven sorrows are:

(1) The first sorrow: the prophecy of Simeon (Hail Mary).
(2) The second sorrow: the flight into Egypt (Hail Mary).
(3) The third sorrow: the loss of the Child Jesus in the temple (Hail Mary).
(4) The fourth sorrow: Jesus and Mary meet on the way to the cross (Hail Mary).
(5) The fifth sorrow: Jesus dies on the cross (Hail Mary).
(6) The sixth sorrow: Jesus is taken down from the cross and laid in Mary's arms (Hail Mary).
(7) The seventh sorrow: the burial of Jesus (Hail Mary).

7. **Litany of the Blessed Virgin Mary.**
Lord, have mercy on us.
Christ, have mercy on us.
Lord, have mercy on us. Christ, hear us.
Christ, graciously hear us.
God, the Father of heaven, *have mercy on us.*
God, the Son, Redeemer of the world, *have mercy on us.*
God, the Holy Spirit, *have mercy on us.*
Holy Trinity, one God, *have mercy on us.*
Holy Mary, *pray for us* (repeat after each invocation).

Holy Mother of God,
Holy Virgin of virgins,
Mother of Christ,
Mother of the Church,
Mother of divine grace,
Mother most pure,
Mother most chaste,
Mother inviolate,
Mother undefiled,
Mother most amiable,
Mother most admirable,
Mother of good counsel,
Mother of our Creator,
Mother of our Savior,
Virgin most prudent,
Virgin most venerable,
Virgin most renowned,
Virgin most powerful,
Virgin most merciful,
Virgin most faithful,
Mirror of justice,
Seat of wisdom,
Cause of our joy,
Spiritual vessel,
Vessel of honor,
Singular vessel of devotion,
Mystical rose,
Tower of David,
Tower of ivory,
House of gold,
Ark of the Covenant,
Gate of heaven,
Morning star,
Health of the sick,
Refuge of sinners,

Comforter of the afflicted,
Help of Christians,
Queen of angels,
Queen of patriarchs,
Queen of prophets,
Queen of apostles,
Queen of martyrs,
Queen of confessors,
Queen of virgins,
Queen of all saints,
Queen conceived without original sin,
Queen assumed into heaven,
Queen of the most holy rosary,
Queen of families,
Queen of peace,
Lamb of God, who take away the sins of the world,
spare us, O Lord.
Lamb of God, who take away the sins of the world,
graciously hear us, O Lord.
Lamb of God, who take away the sins of the world,
have mercy on us.
Pray for us, O holy Mother of God,
that we may be made worthy of the promises of Christ.

Let us pray: Grant, we beseech You, O Lord God, that we Your servants may enjoy perpetual health of mind and body and, by the glorious intercession of the blessed Mary, ever virgin, be delivered from present sorrow, and obtain eternal joy. Through Christ our Lord. Amen.

We fly to your patronage, O holy Mother of God. Despise not our petitions in our necessities, but deliver us always from all dangers, O glorious and blessed Virgin. Amen.

8. **Prayer to St. Joseph.** St. Joseph, guardian of Jesus and

chaste spouse of Mary, you passed your life in perfect fulfillment of duty. You supported the Holy Family of Nazareth with the work of your hands. Kindly protect those who trustingly turn to you. You know their aspirations, their hardships, their hopes; and they turn to you because they know you will understand and protect them. You too have known trial, labor, and weariness. But, even amid the worries of material life, your soul was filled with deep peace and sang out in true joy through intimacy with the Son of God entrusted to you, and with Mary, His tender Mother. Amen.

— *(Pope John XXIII)*

9. **Litany of the Sacred Heart, promises of the Sacred Heart.**
Lord, have mercy on us.
Christ, have mercy on us.
Lord, have mercy on us. Christ, hear us.
Christ, graciously hear us.
God the Father of heaven,
have mercy on us (repeat after each invocation).
God the Son, Redeemer of the world,
God the Holy Spirit,
Holy Trinity, one God,
Heart of Jesus, Son of the eternal Father,
Heart of Jesus, formed by the Holy Spirit in the womb of the Virgin Mother,
Heart of Jesus, substantially united to the Word of God,
Heart of Jesus, of infinite majesty,
Heart of Jesus, sacred temple of God,
Heart of Jesus, tabernacle of the Most High,
Heart of Jesus, house of God and gate of heaven,
Heart of Jesus, burning furnace of charity,
Heart of Jesus, abode of justice and love,
Heart of Jesus, full of goodness and love,
Heart of Jesus, abyss of all virtues,

Heart of Jesus, most worthy of all praise,
Heart of Jesus, king and center of all hearts,
Heart of Jesus, in whom are all the treasures of wisdom
and knowledge,
Heart of Jesus, in whom dwells the fullness of divinity,
Heart of Jesus, in whom the Father is well pleased,
Heart of Jesus, of whose fullness we have all
received,
Heart of Jesus, desire of the everlasting hills,
Heart of Jesus, patient and most merciful,
Heart of Jesus, enriching all who invoke You,
Heart of Jesus, fountain of life and holiness,
Heart of Jesus, propitiation for our sins,
Heart of Jesus, loaded down with opprobrium,
Heart of Jesus, bruised for our offenses,
Heart of Jesus, obedient even to death,
Heart of Jesus, pierced with a lance,
Heart of Jesus, source of all consolation,
Heart of Jesus, our life and reconciliation,
Heart of Jesus, victim of sin,
Heart of Jesus, salvation of those who hope in You,
Heart of Jesus, hope of those who die in You,
Heart of Jesus, delight of all the saints,
Lamb of God, Who take away the sins of the world,
spare us, O Lord.
Lamb of God, Who take away the sins of the world,
graciously hear us, O Lord.
Lamb of God, Who take away the sins of the world,
have mercy on us.
Jesus, meek and humble of heart,
make our hearts like unto Yours.

Let us pray: O almighty and eternal God, look upon
the Heart of Your dearly beloved Son and upon the praise
and satisfaction He offers You in behalf of sinners and,
being appeased, grant pardon to those who seek Your

mercy, in the name of the same Jesus Christ, Your Son, Who lives and reigns with You, in the unity of the Holy Spirit, world without end. Amen.

Promises of Our Lord to those devoted to His Sacred Heart (these should be read by the prayer leader):

(1) I will give them all the graces necessary in their state of life.
(2) I will establish peace in their homes.
(3) I will comfort them in all their afflictions.
(4) I will be their refuge during life and above all in death.
(5) I will bestow a large blessing on all their undertakings.
(6) Sinners shall find in My Heart the source and the infinite ocean of mercy.
(7) Tepid souls shall grow fervent.
(8) Fervent souls shall quickly mount to high perfection.
(9) I will bless every place where a picture of My Heart shall be set up and honored.
(10) I will give to priests the gift of touching the most hardened hearts.
(11) Those who promote this devotion shall have their names written in My Heart, never to be blotted out.
(12) I promise you in the excessive mercy of My Heart that My all-powerful love will grant to all those who communicate on the first Friday in nine consecutive months the grace of final penitence; they shall not die in My disgrace nor without receiving their sacraments; My divine Heart shall be their safe refuge in this last moment.

10. **Prayer for Priests.** "Lord Jesus, Chief Shepherd of the Flock, we pray that in the great love and mercy of Your Sacred Heart You attend to all the needs of Your priest-shepherds throughout the world. We ask that You draw

back to Your Heart all those priests who have seriously strayed from Your path, that You rekindle the desire for holiness in the hearts of those priests who have become lukewarm, and that You continue to give Your fervent priests the desire for the highest holiness. United with Your Heart and Mary's Heart, we ask that You take this petition to Your heavenly Father in the unity of the Holy Spirit. Amen."

11. **Prayer for all members of the Shepherds of Christ Associates.** "Dear Jesus, we ask Your special blessings on all members of Shepherds of Christ Associates. Continue to enlighten them regarding the very special privilege and responsibility you have given them as members of Your movement, Shepherds of Christ Associates. Draw them ever closer to Your Heart and to Your Mother's Heart. Allow them to more and more realize the great and special love of Your Hearts for each of them as unique individuals. Give them the grace to respond to Your love and Mary's love with an increased love of their own. As they dwell in Your Heart and Mary's Heart, abundantly care for all their needs and those of their loved ones. We make our prayer through You to the Father, in the Holy Spirit, with Mary our Mother at our side. Amen."

12. **Prayer for the spiritual and financial success of the priestly newsletter.** "Father, we ask Your special blessings upon the priestly newsletter, Shepherds of Christ. We ask that You open the priest-readers to the graces You wish to give them through this chosen instrument of Your Son. We also ask that You provide for the financial needs of the newsletter and the Shepherds of Christ Associates. We make our prayer through Jesus, in the Holy Spirit, with Mary at our side. Amen."

13. Prayer for all members of the human family.
"Heavenly Father, we ask Your blessings on all Your children the world over. Attend to all their needs. We ask Your special assistance for all those marginalized people, all those who are so neglected and forgotten. United with our Mother Mary, we make this petition to You through Jesus and in the Holy Spirit. Amen."

14. Prayer to St. Michael and our Guardian Angels:
"St. Michael the Archangel, defend us in battle. Be our safeguard against the wickedness and snares of the devil. May God rebuke him, we humbly pray, and do thou, O prince of the heavenly hosts, by the power of God, cast into hell Satan and all the other evil spirits who prowl about the world seeking the ruin of souls. Amen."
"Angel of God, my guardian dear, to whom God's love commits me here, ever this day be at my side, to light and guard, to rule and guide. Amen."

15. Pause for silent, personal prayer. This should last at least five minutes.

16. Act of consecration to the Sacred Heart of Jesus and the Immaculate Heart of Mary.

"Lord Jesus, Chief Shepherd of the flock, I consecrate myself to Your most Sacred Heart. From Your pierced Heart the Church was born, the Church You have called me, as a member of Shepherds of Christ Associates, to serve in a most special way. You reveal Your Heart as a symbol of Your love in all its aspects, including Your most special love for me, whom You have chosen as Your companion in this most important work. Help me to always love You in return. Help me to give myself entirely to You. Help me always to pour out my life in love of God and neighbor! Heart of Jesus, I place my trust in You!

"Dear Blessed Virgin Mary, I consecrate myself to your maternal and Immaculate Heart, this Heart which is symbol of your life of love. You are the Mother of my Savior. You are also my Mother. You love me with a most special love as a member of Shepherds of Christ Associates, a movement created by your Son as a powerful instrument for the renewal of the Church and the world. In a return of love, I give myself entirely to your motherly love and protection. You followed Jesus perfectly. You are His first and perfect disciple. Teach me to imitate you in the putting on of Christ. Be my motherly intercessor so that, through your Immaculate Heart, I may be guided to an ever closer union with the pierced Heart of Jesus, Chief Shepherd of the flock."

17. **Daily Prayers.** All members should say the Holy Spirit prayer daily and make the act of consecration daily. They should also pray the rosary each day. They are encouraged to use the other above prayers as time allows.

Other great books published by Shepherds of Christ Publications

To order any of the following materials please contact us by mail, phone, fax, email or the Internet:

Shepherds of Christ Publications
P.O. Box 627
China, Indiana 47250 USA

Toll free USA: (888) 211-3041
Tel: (812) 273-8405   Fax: (812) 273-3182
Email: info@sofc.org   http://www.sofc.org

Please contact us for *Prayer Manuals* or to begin a Prayer Chapter to pray for the priests, the Church and the world.

C1. *The Word Alive in Our Hearts*
Homilies by the Reverand Joe
Robinson given at St. Boniface
Church in Cincinnati, Ohio. It is
a tremendous honor Fr. Joe has
allowed us to share these great
gifts with you – for greater
holiness and knowing more and
more about God. $10

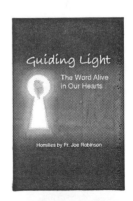

B8. *Mass Book*, by Rita Ring: Many of
the entries in the Priestly
Newsletter Volume II from a
spiritual journal came from this
book. These entries are to help
people to be more deeply united to
God in the Mass. This book is
available in English and Spanish
with the Church's *Imprimatur.* $12

BN3. *Shepherds of Christ - Volume 3* by
Fr. Edward J. Carter, S.J. Contains
Newsletter Issues 1 through 4 of
2000 including Fr. Carter's
tremendous *Overview
of the Spiritual Life* $10

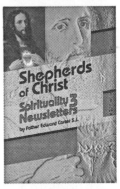

BN2. *Shepherds of Christ - Volume 2*: by
Fr. Edward J. Carter, S.J. Contains
issues 13-29 of the newsletter
(September/October 1996 - Issue
5, 1999) $15

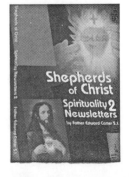

BN1. *Shepherds of Christ - Selected Writings on Spirituality for all People* as Published in Shepherds of Christ Newsletter for Priests. Contains 12 issues of the newsletter from July/August 1994 to May/June 1996. $15

B7. *Rosary Meditations for Parents and Children,* by Rita Ring, Short Meditations for both parents and children to be used when praying the rosary. These meditations will help all to know the lives of Jesus and Mary alive in their Hearts. Available in both English and Spanish with the Church's *Imprimatur.* $10